John H. Muirhead

The Elements of Ethics

an introduction to moral philosophy

John H. Muirhead

The Elements of Ethics
an introduction to moral philosophy

ISBN/EAN: 9783337079529

Printed in Europe, USA, Canada, Australia, Japan

Cover: Foto ©Thomas Meinert / pixelio.de

More available books at **www.hansebooks.com**

THE

ELEMENTS OF ETHICS

AN

INTRODUCTION TO MORAL PHILOSOPHY

BY

J. H. MUIRHEAD, M.A.

LECTURER IN MENTAL AND MORAL SCIENCE, ROYAL HOLLOWAY COLLEGE,
EGHAM; ASSISTANT EXAMINER IN PHILOSOPHY IN THE
UNIVERSITY OF GLASGOW

Τὰ καθήκοντα ὡς ἐπίπαν ταῖς σχέσεσιν παραμετρεῖται
EPICTETUS

*" There is no other genuine enthusiasm for humanity than one which
has travelled the common highway of reason—the life of the good neighbour and the honest citizen—and can never forget that it is still only a
further stage of the same journey."*—T. H. GREEN

NEW YORK

CHARLES SCRIBNER'S SONS

1895

TO

MY UNIVERSITY EXTENSION.

AND OTHER STUDENTS,

THIS HANDBOOK IS INSCRIBED

PREFACE

THIS manual has been written with a special view to the wants and difficulties of University Extension students, to whom, in the first instance, the substance of it was given in a course of lectures. Though attempting to deal with the most recent phases of ethical problems, it does not profess to treat them in an original manner, but merely to apply to their solution ideas which, owing to the labours of the best thinkers of our own time and country, are now common property. Those of my readers who are acquainted with the history of thought in the field of Moral Philosophy will readily recognise the debt I owe to the epoch-making writers Plato and Aristotle among the ancients, Kant and Hegel in modern times. Only second to these in importance for the student are their distinguished exponents in Germany and Great Britain, Erdmann, Zeller, T. H. Green, and Professor Edward Caird. For those who are as yet beginners in philosophy, my best hope in writing this manual will be realised if they are stimulated by it to apply themselves to these and other perennial sources of ethical inspiration.

Students who are familiar with recent continental literature on the subject may be surprised at the absence of all allusion to the ethical writings of Wundt, Steinthal, Paulsen, Höffding, and others. The reason of this omission, as well as of the general character of the references, has been my desire not to burden a book which is meant for a special class of English readers with references to authors to whom they may not have ready access.

In the preparation of these sheets for the press, besides the assistance I have obtained from the Editor of this series, I have to acknowledge my obligations to Mr. J. S. Mackenzie, of Trinity College, Cambridge, whose criticisms upon the proof I found extremely valuable. But my chief thanks are due to Miss M. S. Gilliland, who read the whole of my manuscript and made many helpful suggestions, both as to the matter and the form of treatment.

LONDON, *January*, 1892.

CONTENTS

ix

BOOK II

MORAL JUDGMENT

CHAPTER I

THE OBJECT OF MORAL JUDGMENT

CHAPTER II

THE STANDARD OF MORAL JUDGMENT—MORAL LAW

BOOK III

THEORIES OF THE END

CHAPTER I

THE END AS PLEASURE

CHAPTER II

THE END AS SELF-SACRIFICE

Contents

CHAPTER III

EVOLUTIONARY HEDONISM

BOOK IV

THE END AS GOOD

CHAPTER I

THE END AS COMMON GOOD

CHAPTER II

FORMS OF THE GOOD

BOOK V

MORAL PROGRESS

CHAPTER I

THE STANDARD AS RELATIVE

CHAPTER II

THE STANDARD AS PROGRESSIVE

CHAPTER III

THE STANDARD AS IDEAL

BOOK I

THE SCIENCE OF ETHICS

CHAPTER 1

§ 1. How can there be a Problem at all?

PHILOSOPHY, said Plato, begins in wonder. The child who wonders why her wax doll shuts its eyes, or her kitten wags its tail, has already set forward on the path that leads to philosophy and science. The differences among us that distinguish learned from ignorant depend merely upon the extent to which we have carried our wonder; whether we are content to acquiesce in superficial answers, or still find our wonder unsatisfied, and press on with a new question so soon as our first is answered. Thus, astronomy begins in the wonder and perplexity caused by the contradictions and confusions of the apparent movements of the heavens. The various systems that have succeeded one another—the Ptolemaic, the Copernican, the Newtonian—have differed only in the relative satisfactoriness of the solutions they have offered. The question I propose to discuss in this chapter is, What kind of wonder is that in which Ethics begins? To what does that wonder attach? How does it first rise? How does it express itself? The question of the precise subject-matter of ethics is deferred. Here I would ask why should there be a science of ethics at all, rather

3

than what the science of ethics is. It may, indeed, seem absurd to ask why it should exist before we know what it is. But in this case the "what" is a good deal determined by the "why." At the same time, it must be admitted that some of the definitions and results, reached in a later part of this treatise, are taken for granted in this chapter and the next.

Etymologies rarely help us much in acquiring accurate conceptions of the present use of words. They are as often as not misleading.* In the present case, etymology will give us considerable help. Ethics is precisely what its derivation (ἦθος) implies, the science of moral character. We are, moreover, further helped if we carry our etymology a step further back, and recollect that ἦθος is connected with ἔθος, custom or habit. Similarly, if we revert to the older name under which our science was known, viz., Moral Philosophy,† we find that this means the philosophy of *mores*, which signifies in Latin, primarily customs or habits, secondarily the habits of moral agents in respect to moral action, *i.e.*, character. Assuming, then, that ethics is the science of character, and that character means, according to its etymology, customs or habits of conduct,‡ our question is, How does that "wonder," which is the source of all science, come to attach to national and individual habits of conduct?

* *E.g.*, any one who should define Politics, in terms of its etymology, as the science of civil life, and should go on to argue that politicians were those who possessed this science, would clearly make a great mistake. Whately (*Logic.* p. 118) would convict him of the " Fallacy of Etymology."

† Compare " Physics " and " Natural Philosophy."

‡ "Character," in our modern view, carries with it greater inwardness than this definition seems to contain. This is quite in conformity with the more subjective aspect which all questions of

The very statement of this question suggests a diffi
culty. For at first it might appear as though habitual
actions were just that part of conduct which had
ceased to perplex us or cause us any trouble. All
habits can be shown psychologically to be themselves
the completed form of answers to practical problems.
The habit of moving one's limbs in walking is the
solution of the problem of balancing oneself first
on one leg and then on another, and executing a
forward movement at the same time.* When it has
become a *habit*, the solution is complete. We are no
longer troubled with the problem; we are not even conscious that it is one. Similarly with habits of *conduct*
in a nation or individual. The habit, for instance, of
self-restraint in matters of the body, which the ancients
called Temperance, is the solution of the problem of the
relative claims to satisfaction of apparently contradictory
impulses, *e.g.*, the impulse of a man to go to the public-
house, and the impulse to go home to his wife. As a
habit, or element of character, it is that solution carried
to perfection, so that the perfectly temperate man is
no longer conscious of any conflict or problem as he
passes the tavern.

There may, of course, still rise questions as to the
details of the conduct determined by the habit. Thus
it may remain for the temperate man to decide how
much he may drink, at what time, what kind of liquor,
and so on. But these are not ethical questions in the

ethics assume in modern discussions as compared with ancient.
Here it is immaterial whether we define character as habit of conduct or as habit of *will*. See below, p. 52.

* That this is an acquired art any one can see who watches
a baby's ineffectual efforts on the nursery floor.

sense above referred to. They are a matter of insight in the circumstances of a particular case, corresponding to the questions of when, how far, and how fast we shall walk. A hundred such questions may rise in a man's mind in a day, without ever bringing him face to face with the ethical question proper. This latter does not refer primarily to the details of an act under a habit, but to the habit itself. It is not, What acts are just, courageous, temperate? but, What is justice, courage, temperance? And so the difficulty recurs: How can habits of conduct, which are themselves solutions of practical problems in the life of a nation or an individual, ever become the subject of that doubt and perplexity from which science springs?

The answer briefly is, that so long as the solutions are adequate to the existing circumstances, *i.e.*, so long as there is a congruity between the habits of conduct of a nation or individual and the practical problems of life, so long the ethical question remains in abeyance. On the other hand, it is the appearance of new problems, of which the early habits offer no solution, that first throws doubt upon the validity of custom. To see how this is, let us consider the several stages into which, in this respect, the life of progressive nations naturally falls.

§ 2. General Description of the Conditions under which the Problem rises

For the purpose in hand we might divide these stages into three. First, there is the period of the formation of moral habits of a people, the growth of its morality. This corresponds in the individual's life to the period of childhood and early youth. It is the period of its

education.* Next we have the period of action, corresponding to early manhood. This is the period in
which a balance or equilibrium has been established
between the various forces that reside within the
nation. Externally, this equilibrium exhibits itself in
the harmony of classes, the "balance of the constitution," the reconciliation of interests. Internally, it
means the adequacy of the moral aptitudes and habits
of the people, both in force and variety, to meet the
calls of its daily life. The habits, which in the previous stage were, so to speak, in the gristle, have now
hardened into a system of traditional morality, the
maxims of which are embodied in the received moral
code, and entrenched behind national institutions of State
and Church. I have called this the age of action,
because it corresponds generally to the period of a
nation's best energies and most brilliant achievements.
Civil discord is meantime at an end, and the nation is
thus left free to expand its power abroad.† Lastly, we
have the stage of reflection. The balance of internal
powers, which was the characteristic feature of the second
stage, is undermined by the development of new forces.
Chief among these is the intellectual progress that has
gone hand in hand with the enlargement of the nation's

* The mode of this education—the evolution of moral habits
under the pressure of social necessity; the rise of institutions of
family, state, and church, corresponding to them; and the embodiment of directions for their maintenance in moral and legal codes
—would require separate treatment, for which this is clearly not
the place.

† As examples of this stage might be mentioned the Jewish
nation in the time of David, the Athenians in the age of Pericles,
the Romans after the establishment of internal peace by the settle-
ment of the long-standing quarrel between patricians and plebeians.

experience, as its power extended. Corresponding to
this progress will be the rise of new interests, industrial,
literary, artistic, philosophical. These have to find a
place for themselves in the national life. This they can
usually only do at the expense of existing habits, institutions, and formulas. The new wine *has* to be poured
into the old bottles. The spirit is contrary to the form.
A period of intellectual and political ferment sets in; the
age is marked by doubt, perplexity, and hesitation; it is
disconcerted by the apparent baselessness of the forms
and institutions upon which society has hitherto seemed
to rest; the moral law, the fabric of the constitution,
religion itself, seem shaken to their foundations; the
only choice seems to be either to close one's eyes.to the
contradictions of the present, and seek refuge in the old
habits of faith, or to set forward on a new, untried path
of revolution and anarchy.

But this is an alternative which cannot fail to startle
and repel. To admit it is to prove traitor to the intelligence which discerned the new problem, and therefore
in the last resort to morality itself, which, as we have
seen, is only another name for the solution of problems
which once were new. It is at this stage that recourse
is had to Ethics, which opens a third alternative between
simple acceptance and simple rejection of the morality
and institutions of the past. Ethics proposes to try to
understand them. It asks whence they came, and what
they mean. It blinks no difficulty which the spirit
of scepticism suggests. It ignores no claim which tradition puts forward. But it goes its own way, regardless
of both, with a deeper doubt than scepticism, because it
doubts the conclusions of scepticism, and a deeper faith
than traditionalism, because it believes in the reason

which traditions embody, and which is the source of
what power they still possess.

§ 3. Historical Illustration from the Case of Greece

Historically, the best illustration, both of the decomposition of national habits and traditions, owing to the
growth of national life, and of the rise out of this
decomposition of a rational system of morals and
polity, founded upon the effort to understand current
forms and, by revealing both their value and their
inadequacy, to prepare the way for progress—is to
be found in the actual origin of the science of ethics
in the age of the Sophists in Greece. This is not
the place to give any detailed account of the state
of opinion out of which the great systems of Plato and
Aristotle grew.* It is sufficient, in illustration of what
has been already said, to remind the reader that the
Sophists lived at a time of great political, industrial, and
intellectual expansion. Athens, from a small city state,
had become the head of a great empire. New ideas,
new interests, new demands, had produced a vague rest-
lessness and dissatisfaction with older forms of thought
and life. In the hands of the Sophists the criticism
which was the life and breath of the time spread from
attacks on external forms and abstract theories to the
ideas of right and wrong, justice and injustice, piety and
impiety. By their means a general sense of the contradictions that were latent in the traditional morality came
to pervade the educated classes in Athens. A condition
of doubt, uncertainty, and general perplexity was created,

---

* See Sidgwick's *History of Ethics ;* Grant's *Aristotle*, Vol. I.,
Essay ii.; Erdmann's *History of Philosophy*, Vol. I., pp. 69 foll.

out of which in due time rose, under the influence of
Socrates, the first sketch of a science of morality.

§ 4. Illustration from Our Own Time

But we do not require to go to Athens in the time
of the Sophists to find an illustration of the rise of a
science of ethics. Our own time, resembling the age
just referred to in many other respects, resembles it
in nothing more than this—that it is a time of moral
and political unrest, resulting in a new demand among
large numbers of the educated classes to understand
the meaning of the moral code under which they live,
and the institutions that support it. To mention only
a few of the contradictions and seemingly irreconcil-
able antitheses which criticism has made apparent, and
which harass and perplex our age, there is, in the
first place, in the field of religion, the opposition between faith and reason, science and religion, authority
and private judgment. In politics there is the antithesis between the individual and the state. On the one
side are asserted "the rights of man," on the other
"the duties of citizenship." "Man *versus* State "* is
the *cause célèbre* of the century. Coming to more distinctly moral questions, we have the conflict between self
and others, self-interest and the greatest happiness of
the greatest number, pleasure and duty, freedom and
necessity, law and liberty, and other sharp-horned
dilemmas that start from the ground of our common
life when the light of criticism is turned upon it.

For all these and similar contradictions no solution is
possible, except upon condition of a thorough-going

* See Mr. Spencer's booklet with this title.

analysis of the basis of individual and social morality, the origin, the meaning, the authority of the moral habits of civilised man, and the social, political, and religious institutions in which they have entrenched themselves. It is under pressure of these and kindred difficulties that the science of ethics has taken a new start in our own time. It is indeed true that ethics has always been more or less studied in modern times as a department of philosophy. Under its older name of moral philosophy it has always had an honoured place in systems of metaphysics. What is characteristic of our time in this regard is not the rise of a new study, but the new significance that has come to attach to an old one. The practical importance of the science of ethics, as offering valuable aid towards the solution of problems that vex our daily life, has come to be more fully recognised. Among other evidences of this recognition may be mentioned the rise of societies to promote its study,* the institution of the *International Journal of Ethics*, and generally the place that is now claimed for it as no longer a subordinate branch of philosophy, but an independent science.† The validity of this latter claim I shall have occasion hereafter to examine.‡ Meantime it may be noted as an illustration of the new importance attaching to the study that attempts have been made to detach it from the cumbrous adjuncts of logic and metaphysics, and to present it as a science in no respect

---

* There are Ethical Societies in London, Cambridge, Edinburgh, New York, Philadelphia, Chicago, and elsewhere, all of recent growth.

† On the general question of the dissolution of the ancient partnership between philosophy and its various branches, see the excellent article by James Ward, *Mind*, Vol. XV., No. 58.

‡ See pp. 28 foll.

differing, save in the complexity of its subject-matter
and the practical importance of its conclusions, from
other empirical sciences.*

§ 5. Effect of the Study of Ethics on our General View of Life

If now, reverting to our definition of ethics as the
science of moral habits, the reader ask what we may
expect to be the general effect of such an investigation
on our general view of the nature and authority of these
habits, I answer that that effect will be twofold. First,
it will necessarily be partly destructive. This is implied
in saying that science is critical. It criticises, corrects,
supplements, and classifies the distinctions of common-
sense. All science does this: it is a criticism of
common-sense. Ethical science will be found to do so
specifically. Some familiar distinctions, some effete
prohibitions and injunctions, some crude notions of the
nature of moral authority and moral sanctions, will have
to be given up. For moral law, like statute law, grows by
constant alteration and accretion. As these alterations
and accretions take place more or less unconsciously,
little care is taken to revise and readjust what went
before. And just as many contradictory laws, passed at
various times, without reference to one another, may
remain on the statute book, so the moral code of any
period may contain many elements loosely compacted
and imperfectly reconciled with one another. The
result of the application of scientific criticism to these
will be like the revisal and codification of statute law.

* See Leslie Stephen's *Science of Ethics*, pp. 6, 7. Also S.
Alexander's *Moral Order and Progress*, p. 80.

Similarly, in reference to the social institutions that support the moral law, we may expect that our results will have a negative and critical side. These also, like the moral code, are an unconscious growth. Like the organs of animal life, they were evolved in response to vital needs. Yet, as there are survivals and rudimentary organs among the parts of animals, so in a community forms and institutions may survive from a former state of life. One of the first results of ethical science will be the perception of this fact.

Lastly, with regard to the authority on which the moral law is based, we may expect, in the first instance, a critical and apparently negative result. As man's notions of this authority were formed in the ages of poetry and mythology, we may expect the ordinary notions about it to be tinged with the colour of their origin. It is a necessary part of the work of science to criticise them. In all these respects, science "is nothing if it is not critical."

On the other hand, ethics has a positive and reconstructive side. To explain is not to explain away, neither is to explain away to explain. Its starting-point is the reality of duty and right. If in its first *rôle* as critical it seems to be attacking these, this is only the superficial aspect of its work.* In its deeper aspect it is reconstructive. It comes, not to destroy, but to fulfil. It does so by separating the essential from the unessential, the permanent from the transient, the spirit from the form of moral and social institutions. By leaving only those which are organically connected with human

---

* In all scientific education there is a stage in which destruction seems to be the chief work of science. Plato calls it the "puppy dog" stage.

nature and with one another, it gives them a value and a sanctity which, as merely traditional forms, they never could possess. Ethics is thus a criticism which makes reconstruction possible: it strips off the irrelevant and the unessential, in order to get a firmer hold of the essential. Here and there it presents us with a bold negative, but, when it does so, this is found only to be "the cutting edge of a positive."

CHAPTER II

CAN THERE BE A SCIENCE OF ETHICS?

§ 6. Difficulty in the Conception of such a Science

In the preceding chapter a sketch has been given of the circumstances in which the practical need for a science of ethics arises, the general nature of its problem, and the kind of answer to it that may be expected. We have now to seek for a convenient starting-point in developing the science itself. But before we do so several preliminary difficulties that rise in connection with the very idea of a science of this kind require to be noticed.

Accepting the general definition (given on p. 4) of ethics as the science of character or conduct, in what sense, we may ask, can we speak of such a science? Science, it is said, has for its subject-matter necessary truths. It traces effects to their causes, formulates general laws as to the way in which these causes act, and from these generalisations, or the combinations of them, proceeds to deduce new consequences. The last of these processes is especially distinctive of a science. No science is considered complete until it is shown to be possible to predict particular effects from the known laws of their causes. According to this idea of a science, it becomes at once evident that, in assuming the possibility of a science of character and conduct, we assume that these phenomena are the effects of certain definable causes, that it is possible to formulate general laws of their origin and course of development, and that when the science is perfected we shall be able to make confident predictions regarding them on the ground of our previous generalisations. Thus at the very outset we seem to make certain assumptions as to the nature of human character and conduct, the discussion of which has always been one of the chief subjects of moral philosophy. For is it not contended by a large and powerful school of writers that "character and conduct are precisely that which cannot be explained as the resultant of discernible and calculable forces? They are chiefly dependent upon the human will, and we have no right at the outset of our investigation to make an assumption which prejudges the question as to the free-dom of volition. If the will is free, the whole conception of a science of ethics falls to the ground: there is a variable and incalculable element in character and conduct which vitiates all its results."

This objection is, however, based upon a miscon-ception of the nature of the science. It is indeed possible to treat human conduct as a natural phenom-enon on the same plane as other physical events, such as the motions of the planets, or the evolution of species. The aim of the science upon this supposition will be to formulate general laws of the action of human agents in specific circumstances, and thence deduce the course it will take in nations and individuals upon the recurrence of the same conditions. A science of this kind, difficult as it might prove to be to work it out in detail, is at least conceivable, and it would

certainly proceed upon the assumption that the freedom
of the will is a delusion, or at any rate may be neglected
for purposes of the science. But such a science would
have little or nothing to do with ethics. Ethics is not
primarily concerned with *conduct as a fact in space and
time*,—something done here and now, following from
certain causes in the past, and succeeded by certain
results in the future. It is concerned with the *judgment
upon conduct*, the judgment that such and such conduct is
right or wrong. The distinction is important, and may be
made the basis of a general classification of the sciences.
On the one hand, we have those sciences which are concerned with facts or phenomena of nature or of mind,
actual occurrences which have to be analysed, classified,
and explained. The movement of the earth round the
sun is such a fact. Astronomy may be taken as the type
of this class of sciences. On the other hand, there are
those sciences which have to do primarily, not with facts
in space and time, but with judgments about those facts.
It might be said, indeed, that all facts present themselves
to us as judgments. "The earth moves round the sun"
is a fact, but it is also a judgment. There is a distinction,
however (to go no deeper), between a judgment *of* fact
and a judgment *upon* fact, corresponding to the distinction between "judgment" in its logical sense of "proposition" and "judgment" in its judicial sense of "sentence."
It is with judgment in the latter sense that ethics has to
do. It deals with conduct as the subject of judicial judgment, not with conduct merely as a physical fact. Similarly it might be argued that all judgments are facts, and
that a moral judgment only differs from other facts in
being more complicated. This of course is true, but one
of the chief elements in this complication is the refer-

ence to a standard, and it is this element to which I wish
to call attention as distinctive of the fact with which
our science has to deal. On the ground of it ethics has
to be classed with what have been called "normative"
sciences, to which Logic, or the science of the judgment
of truth or falsity, and .Esthetics, or the science of the
judgment of beauty or ugliness, belong. Ethics has to do
with the norm, or standard of right and wrong, as logic
has to do with the standard of truth, æsthetics with the
standard of beauty. It is concerned primarily with the
laws that regulate our judgments of right and wrong, only
secondarily with the laws that regulate conduct as an
event in time.

§ 7. Practical Difficulty in the Conception of a Science of Conduct

There is a second objection that may be taken to
such a science from the practical side. It has been
said that ethics is the science of the laws which regulate
our judgments of right and wrong. But how then, it
may be asked, does it come about that the great mass
of people who are perfectly innocent of such a science,
yet confidently pass such judgments on themselves and
others? It is these judgments of ordinary people, moreover, from which presumably the science of ethics proposes to start, and it is these it proposes to investigate.
But what hope can there be of finding any law or reason
embodied in popular judgments, obviously arrived at
without any relation to laws of judgment previously
known and acted upon?

The answer to this difficulty has already been given
in the previous chapter. The objection springs from the

failure to distinguish between an unconsciously acquired art, and the science which analyses the principles which underlie it. Just as the art of speaking or of reasoning may be acquired by those who have never seen or heard of a book on grammar or logic, so the art of moral judgment and moral conduct may be acquired by the unconscious processes described above (p. 5) before a science of ethics is even dreamt of. How far the science of conduct will react upon the art, what influence ethics has on morality, is another question. The kind of answer that may be expected to be given to it has already been alluded to (pp. 12 foll.). In the present section I desire merely to emphasise a distinction which, though so obvious when stated, is obscured in current language.

§ 8. What may be Expected of a Science of Ethics?

If we now come closer to the question of the present chapter, and ask in what sense there can be said to be a science of moral judgment, we open up a still more serious difficulty. Although the full import of our answer can only be apprehended after the claim that is now to be made on behalf of ethics has been justified by the detailed exposition of the theory itself, still it may be permissible to state here generally what we may expect as the result of the present inquiry.

Before attempting to do so, it is necessary, however, to define more clearly than we have yet done what a science in the strict sense is, and what we require that it should do for us. Let us take astronomy as our type, and ask, Wherein does the scientific differ from the ordinary way of looking at things? In the first place, it *observes accurately*. In astronomy

every one knows that the heavenly bodies change their
position with reference to the earth and one another.
Science demands, in the first place, accurate observations
and descriptions of these changes. Secondly, science
distinguishes different kinds of the phenomena thus
observed, and *classifies* them according to their most
significant differences. It will, for instance, in astronomy
very soon arrive at the distinction between our own sun
and planetary system, and more distant suns. Within
this it will distinguish moons from planets, planets that
have cooled sufficiently to permit of life upon their
surface from those that have not, and so on. But if its
functions ended here, it would hardly merit the name of
a science at all. It must not only accurately observe
and classify: it must *explain*. Without entering into
any detailed discussion of what is meant by "explanation," which is a question for logic, not for ethics, I may
define shortly what I wish the reader to understand by
this term. To explain a phenomenon or occurrence, in
the proper sense of the term, it is not sufficient, as popular
language implies, to find the cause or agency which produced it. Even the account given by the older books
on logic, which define explanation as the process of
finding a more general law, or more general laws, under
which the occurrence may be subsumed, is inadequate.*
Explanation includes this, but is not exhausted by it.
A thing can only properly be said to be explained when
it is seen necessarily to flow from the sum of the conditions which the science in question takes into account.
But these conditions, when accurately apprehended, are
never merely a series of successive phenomena, but

---

* For this kind of explanation in its three forms, see Mill's
Logic, Book III., ch. xii.; Bain's *Inductive Logic*, Book III., ch. xii.

the relations of the parts or members of an *organic system* to one another. Hence we may substitute for this definition a still more accurate one, and say that a phenomenon is only fully explained when enough is known of the particular system in question to permit us to apprehend the phenomenon in the light of the known relations of the other parts, and therefore as a coherent member of the whole. Thus, to take a simple instance, the phenomenon of the dawn is explained in the sense described when we see it to be the necessary result of the sum of conditions which we know as the planetary system; in other words, when we know enough of the mutual relations of the various members of the planetary system, and the laws of their motions, to see that these involve the turning of our part of the earth to the light of the sun at a particular moment in the manner we call the sunrise.*

By this third stage, therefore, in the scientific account of any phenomenon, we mean the process by which it is shown to be a coherent part of a system or organism. It is shown to be "required" by the conditions previously known to prevail in a particular field or group of facts. As so explained, it is seen to be necessarily involved in these conditions so soon as we realise what they mean; in other words, to be a necessary truth. Of course the particular group is itself related to other groups, and ultimately to the whole system of known reality; so that the complete explanation of

---

* A simple example of this process of explanation would be the adjustment of a piece in a child's picture puzzle. The "explanation" of its apparently strange shape and jumble of coloured surface is only found when its place has been assigned to it in the organic structure of the whole.

any fact requires that we should see it to be necessarily involved in the constitution of the cosmos as
a whole. Science however, quâ Science, contents itself
with the perceived necessity of its data relatively to a
limited sphere, *e.g.*, spatial, mechanical, or chemical relations. On the other hand, the ultimate relations of these
spheres to one another, and to reality as a whole, is the
point of view distinctive of Philosophy, the difference
being that Science, as such, is content with the relatively
complete explanation which consists in showing particular
phenomena to flow necessarily from a particular group of
organic relations, as in astronomy or biology; Philosophy
requires us to see the same fact in organic relation to the
world as a whole.

Returning from this digression, we are now in a position to understand what is meant by the statement that
ethics is a science. It is so, not merely in the sense that
it observes and classifies its data, as in the current tables
of the different forms of moral judgment known as duties;
it also aims at explaining them. Its function is to exhibit
these forms as necessarily flowing from the known conditions of the individual and social life of man. To the
unreflective, moral judgments appear to be somewhat
isolated phenomena, without relation to one another or
to other facts of experience. Upon the field of otherwise strictly correlated and comprehensible facts and
events, there appears to be intruded an arbitrary pro-
nouncement of condemnation or approval. It is the
work of ethics, on the other hand, to bring these
judgments into organic relation with one another and
with the known facts of experience; to strip them of
their apparent arbitrariness, and clothe them with the
livery of reason, by showing them to be necessary

postulates of that organism of relations which we know as human society.

§ 9. Comparison of Ethics as so interpreted with Intuitionist and Theological Ethics

The nature and extent of this claim will be more obvious if we contrast it shortly with two other views that have been held as to the nature and limits of ethical investigation. Attempts have been made to limit the scope of the science to the description and classification of the utterances of what is called Moral Sense. The only ultimate account which we can give, it is said, of those pronouncements as to right and wrong, which we call moral judgments, is that in the presence of certain conditions (*e.g.*, one's neighbour's purse and a desire for money) moral sense pronounces certain judgments (*e.g.*, that it is wrong to take what is not one's own). Ethics has to do with the description and classification of these judgments. It cannot further explain them. They rest upon an innate feeling or instinct that defies further analysis. As against this view we should, of course, admit the existence of what is called moral sense or feeling,—the consideration of which is an important part of ethics,—but we should refuse to regard it as the unanalysable utterance of a special faculty. It has an origin, a history, and a place among the other data of the moral life which it is the function of ethics to unfold. Similarly, its *dicta* (though it is not at all clear how a "sense" can speak as well as feel) are not isolated utterances (as such they would be wholly unintelligible), but derive what significance they have from their relation to an objective system of mutually related parts or elements.

Another view traces the moral judgments or decrees which are the subject-matter of ethics back to the will of an external authority. They are communicated to man partly through conscience, partly through revelation, but in both cases are in the last resort to be explained by a direct reference to this Supreme Will, not to human life and experience as such. It is not necessary to enter on disputed points of theology to see that, whatever the connection between morality and religion (and it is a very close one) may be, this view amounts either to a denial of any science of ethics in the proper sense of the word, or to the logical fallacy of *petitio principii*. If it be meant that no account can be given of the good and the right, except that they are the will of God, there is an end to all inquiry. We may be told by conscience and revelation what is right, but to the question of science, *Why* is it right? *why* am I bound to accept this authority? there is no answer. If, on the other hand, it be meant merely that the good and the right become known to us through the direct action of another will upon our minds and consciences, *i.e.*, that we know that this is right, that wrong, because God tells us, the truth of this account will be a question for theology and metaphysics; but, true or false, it does not help us to the solution of the ethical question. We are still left to ask, Why is it right? Is it right because God wills it, or does God will it because it is right? In the former case we are back at the denial of the possibility of any science of ethics; in the latter case we are still at the beginning of our investigation, and our explanation of the judgment of right is still to seek.

I claim then for ethics that it is a science in the same sense as any one of the physical or material sciences. It aims at *explaining* moral judgments, as astronomy aims at explaining the motions of the planets, or geometry the properties of figures, by showing their place in a system which cannot exist as a consistent whole (or, in other words, cannot be recognised by reason as existing at all) without them.   Thus, to anticipate, the judgment that theft is wrong is not explained by merely referring it to a moral sense or feeling, or to the decree of a Divine will, but by showing that disregard for other people's property is inconsistent with that system of mutual relations which we call social life.

CHAPTER III

SCOPE OF THE SCIENCE OF ETHICS

§ 10. In what sense Ethics differs from the Natural Sciences

HAVING indicated in what sense ethics may be said to resemble other sciences, it remains for me further to define its general character by pointing out in what respects it differs from them. It differs from all the natural sciences in that:—

(1) *It is regulative.* Ethics deals with a rule or standard of judgment, not with physical events and the causes which determine them. This has been already explained, and need not now detain us. It involves, however, a further distinction which it is of the utmost importance to note.

(2) *It treats man as conscious.* Seeing that ethics deals with judgments consciously passed by man upon himself and others, it rests upon the assumption that man is not merely a part of nature and the blind servant of her purposes, but is *conscious* of being a part, and of being subject to her laws. He not only behaves in a certain way in presence of particular circumstances, as oxygen may be said to "behave" in the presence of hydrogen, but he is conscious of his behaviour in its relation to

himself and others. It is on the ground of this consciousness that he passes judgment upon it. Hence any attempt to treat the science of human conduct and character as merely a branch of material science is doomed to failure. The "explanations" in the field of ethics cannot be in terms of the laws and hypotheses that are applicable in the field of physical science. The laws of motion or the principle of the conservation of force are here out of court. It is true that human conduct may be described as a mode or form of energy, but the important thing is the "form,"—it is *conscious* energy, and that makes all the difference. Nothing has created more confusion in the history of science than the attempt to take principles which successfully explain phenomena in one field and apply them to those of another to which they are inapplicable. It was thus that the Pythagoreans thought that the laws of abstract number were adequate to explain the concrete facts of the physical world; the atomists that the hypothesis of indestructible, material atoms, was sufficient to explain all phenomena of life and thought. And though we have given over these attempts in their cruder forms, yet we are still liable, in our enthusiasm for a principle which we have victoriously applied in one field, to overlook fundamental distinctions of subject-matter, and apply it in a field where it is either altogether irrelevant or only relatively valid.* We are in continual danger of forgetting that the world does not consist of groups of facts all upon the same plane and explicable by

---

* As a prominent instance of this mistake at the present time we might take the tendency to apply the law of natural selection, as it is observed to operate in unconscious nature and among the lower animals, to the life of man as a conscious and intelligent

the same axioms and definitions, but disposes them in
an ascending series resembling rather a spiral column,
from each new round of which we view the facts that
lie before us from a higher plane and at a different
angle. In regard to ethics we may here so far anticipate
as to state the view, hereafter to be proved, that it differs
from the sciences that stand next below it, viz., biology
and natural history, in that while these treat man as
organically related to his environment in nature and
society, ethics treats of him as. conscious of that
relation.

(3) *It is more closely related to philosophy.* Another
distinction is important. It flows naturally from the
two already mentioned. It has already been observed
(p. 22) that the explanations of particular sciences are,
after all, relative. No fact or phenomenon is fully
explained till its relations to all the world beside are
clearly known and defined. But all the world beside,
or the whole system of things, is not the subject-matter
of any particular science. So far as it can be made
a subject of investigation at all, it is the subject of
philosophy or metaphysics, the science of sciences.*
But while philosophy alone deals with complete or final
explanations, yet relatively, and in their own field, the
explanations of the particular sciences are regarded as
valid. It might be said, for instance, that the truth

member of a social system. Even Mr. Spencer is not altogether
free from this error. A great deal of the antagonism to the scientific
treatment of the moral life is probably due to attempts to explain its
phenomena upon inadequate principles.

* Which, however, ought not to be thought of as opposed to the
sciences, but only as " an unusually obstinate effort to think clearly "
on their subject-matter.

of the fifth proposition of the first book of Euclid
is independent of the conclusions of philosophy as to
the nature and reality of space, and no one would
think it worth while seriously to question the statement that mathematics is independent of metaphysics.
But the question may be and has been put with reference
to ethics, Is it in like manner independent of philosophy?
The older thinkers apparently were of opinion that it
was not, as it was commonly spoken of as moral *philosophy*. Modern nomenclature and methods of treating
it have emphasised its independence.   Recent writers
even go out of their way to disown all connection between
ethics and metaphysics.   But besides the general connection which there is between all the sciences which
deal with some particular aspect of the world (*e.g.*, mathematics, which deals with space: dynamics, which deals
with bodies in motion) and philosophy or metaphysics,
which deals with the nature and reality of the world as a
whole, there is in the case of ethics a more particular
connection.   This is manifest whether we take the point
of view of the first or of the second of the distinctions
already mentioned.

For (*a*) *its judgments are thought to be absolute*.
Ethics, we have seen, has to do with moral judgments,
and these judgments are judgments of value—the value
of conduct or character.   Now, whatever they be in
reality, they are apparently, at least, judgments of absolute, not merely of relative value; for it is usually
thought and asserted that conduct is good or bad, not
merely relatively, *i.e.*, according as we choose to regard
a certain end (*e.g.*, the good of the society in which
we live) as desirable or not, but absolutely, *i.e.*, without
relation to our individual views of what is desirable

or not desirable in particular circumstances. This apparently is the meaning of duty and right as contrasted with pleasure or utility. In other words, morality is commonly thought to be required by the nature of things as a whole, not merely by the circumstances in which we happen to live. It is not necessary here to decide whether this opinion is true or false. Clearly if it is true there is a most intimate connection between ethics and metaphysics. And even if it be false it is difficult to see how its falsity can be proved without more or less overt reference to a philosophical doctrine of the place of man in the universe, and his relation to its central principle and purpose.

(*b*) *Man's consciousness of himself as a member of society involves a reference to a cosmic order.* This intimate connection between ethics and metaphysics may further be illustrated from the fact that in the former we have to do, not only with man as related to his material and social environment, but with man as conscious of this relationship. For this consciousness, as may be easily shown, involves a reference to the whole world besides, as a cosmos or order in which he has a place. In being conscious of himself as a citizen of a particular state, or as a member of the human brotherhood, he is also conscious of himself as a citizen of the world and as a member of a cosmos of related beings. And just as it is impossible to think of himself as a member of any lesser circle of relations, *e.g.*, of the family, without thinking of himself as a member of a larger circle, *e.g.*, a society or state, so it is impossible to think of himself as a member of society without thinking of himself as a member of a universal or cosmic order. His thought of himself, moreover, in this latter aspect, overflows, as it were, into all his other thoughts about himself, transforming and moulding them in such a way that it is impossible to treat of any of the lower forms of consciousness, *e.g.*, his social consciousness, without taking the higher into account. It is of course possible for the moment and for purposes of science to abstract one aspect or form of consciousness, such as the consciousness of ourselves as members of a particular society, from our consciousness of ourselves in general, just as it is possible to abstract a particular form or aspect of space or of force from space or force in general. But when we come to analyse our social consciousness into its constituent elements, and ask, as we do in ethics, What is its nature and contents? we find that the answer depends upon our answer to the wider question, as to the nature and contents of consciousness as a whole, in a far more intimate way than does the question of the properties of the triangle or the electric current upon the question of the nature of space or force in general. Thus, to take a single instance, the science of mathematics will remain unaffected whether we believe with one school of metaphysicians that our knowledge of space is given from without, or with another that it is an *a priori* form contributed by the mind itself. But no one could say that our ethical analysis of that form of social consciousness which we call conscience will remain unaffected whether we believe with the Epicureans that the world is an accidental concourse of atoms, or hold with the Stoics that it is the reflection of divine intelligence. We are thus led to the conclusion that, while the natural sciences may be said to be practically independent of metaphysics, the conclusions of philosophy as to the nature of the world at large and man's relation to it are of the utmost importance to ethics, and cannot be neglected in a complete exposition of its subject-matter.*

While this is so, it may be convenient and even necessary, in an elementary treatise like the present, to consider the subject-matter of ethics with as little reference as possible to the philosophical questions involved. Little harm can come of this course, so long as we know what we are about. It only comes to be misleading when we confuse the temporary convenience of neglecting these questions with the permanent possibility of doing so. To assert that we may for purposes of investigation abstract from metaphysical considerations is one thing; to assert their irrelevance to our ultimate results is quite another.

§ 11. Ethics as a "Practical" Science

Ethics has sometimes been distinguished from the natural sciences on the ground that it is practical, while they are theoretic. On examination, however, the distinction is found to be a superficial one. It is true, indeed, that ethics stands nearer to our everyday life than do, for instance, astronomy or physiology. Its very name, as we have seen, implies this, and on this ground it has sometimes been called practical philosophy. It is the science of conduct (πρᾶξις) and the judgments which more deeply affect it. Its conclusions may therefore be said to be of immediate and universal interest in a sense which cannot be claimed for the conclusions of the sciences just mentioned. But this does not carry us far. For it may easily be shown that

---

* The precise point at which metaphysical questions press themselves upon our notice will be noted below. See p. 215.

as a science ethics is just as theoretic as astronomy or physiology, while, as furnishing the basis for the scientific practice of the arts, *e.g.*, of navigation and of healing, these sciences are just as practical as ethics.

The idea that there can be such a thing as a science which is purely theoretic comes from our habit of thinking of the natural sciences as systems of truth elaborated in books which are chiefly useful as a means of intellectual training. In the early stages of the history of science such a mistake was impossible. Man's interest in the laws of nature was then only the reflection of his interest in his own ends and purposes. Causes in nature were only interesting as means to practical ends.* It is true that there came a time when man began to develop that "disinterested curiosity" which is the condition of all higher achievement in science. Yet it is equally true that, just in proportion as scientific research becomes divorced from the practical interest that man has in the subjugation of nature, there is a danger that it may become pedantic or dilettanti.† Even the most abstract and theoretic of all the sciences, viz., metaphysics or philosophy, while, as Novalis said, "it bakes no bread," is not without important bearing on the practical problems of everyday life.

On the other hand, the notion that ethics is less theoretic than any other science can only come from

---

* See Höffding's *Psychology*, p. 240 (Eng. Tr.).

† Mr. Casaubon's Key to all Mythologies in *Middlemarch* appears to have been of this character. One cannot help a suspicion that much of the erudition of the present time, which, as Hegel once said, "finds most to be done where there is least to be got from it," is in the same condition. On the whole subject see Note at end of Book IV. below.

the tendency, already remarked upon, to confuse theory with practice in the field of conduct—ideas and judgments *about* morality in the study or in the class-room with moral ideas and moral judgments in the concrete circumstances of daily life.

§ 12. Has Ethics to do with what Ought to be rather than with what Is?

Closely allied with the view just criticised is another that is not less misleading. Ethics, it is said, differs from the natural sciences in that, while they deal with things as they are, ethics deals with them as they ought to be. This distinction, it is maintained, is based upon the fundamental antithesis between natural and moral law. The former is the law of what is, the latter of what is to be.

Now it is undoubtedly true that for the individual the moral law represents something that ought to be, as opposed to physical law, which is a statement of what is. The law of gravitation is a statement of the actual relation between the pen I hold in my hand and the earth which attracts it. On the other hand, the law that I shall be perfectly sincere in the opinions I express by my writing is a statement of what ought to be my relation to my reader, whatever the actual fact may be. But this is no more than to say that, as by this time must be obvious to the student, these two are laws in a wholly different sense. In the one case we have a scientific generalisation from the observation of facts, in the other we have a *rule* or maxim flowing from such a generalisation. What corresponds to moral law in this sense is the practical rule deducible from the conclusions of any particular science, *e.g.*, the rules of health which are deducible from the conclusions of physiology.   On the other hand, what corresponds in ethics to the theoretic conclusions of science are the definitions, classifications, and explanations of which I gave a general account in the preceding chapter.   It is, indeed, true that in the search for the conclusions there sketched out we start from judgments of what ought to be,—this constitutes the distinctive mark of the science,—but it deals with these judgments as actual facts.   At each step, moreover, in its progress the science is, as we shall see, in the closest contact with concrete facts, in just as true a sense as any other science.   Thus it is its aim to show how moral judgments as to what ought to be are always relative to what is; they imply at every point the actual existence of a moral order, apart from which, as it is revealed in social relations, there could be no such thing as a moral law, any more than, apart from the known relations of the bodily organs to one another in what we might call the physiological order which reveals itself in them, there could be any laws of health in the ordinary sense of the term.

In criticising the distinction which it has been sought to establish between ethics and other sciences, on the ground of the difference between the "ought" and the "is," I have not meant to deny or in any way to obliterate the latter antithesis.   However closely these categories may be related to one another, no identification of them is ultimately possible.   I have merely wished to point out that the distinction between them is not applicable as a principle of division among the sciences themselves.*

* See Dewey's *Outlines of Ethics*, pp. 174 foll.

§ 13. Distinction between Ethics and Politics

It remains to distinguish ethics from a science with
which it may seem to have been confused, when we spoke
of the former as having to do with man as a member of
society, namely, politics.* The connection between them
is obvious. They both deal with human conduct and
character. They both treat of these in connection with
the end of human good, and therefore as the subject of
moral judgment. They both conceive of them as subject
to laws, carrying with them judicial rewards and penalties.
The difference is that while ethics is concerned with the
analysis of conduct and character as the subjects of moral
judgment (*i.e.*, as right and wrong), simply, politics has to
do with the analysis of those external forms and institutions which lay down in outline the fields in which right
conduct primarily manifests itself, viz., the family, school,
church, profession, etc. Hence ethics may be said to
precede politics. Only after we have arrived at a clear
conception of the inward nature of right conduct can
we hope to settle the question as to its proper external
conditions. The foundation of a true criticism of

* The word is here used in its ancient and honourable, not in its
somewhat degraded modern sense. Just as " Ethics " is preferred
to the more ambitious title of " Moral Philosophy," so " Politics "
may be preferred to " Political Philosophy," but in both cases it is
to be understood that a science, not an art, is intended. The hybrid
term, " Sociology," seems likely to assert a place for itself. I understand the word as meaning the theory of society in general, inclu ling
its origin and growth, whereas politics is the theory of civilised
society organised as a state. On the distinction between Society
and State, see D. G. Ritchie's *Principles of State Interference*,
Appendix.

political institutions must be laid in a true criticism of human life as subject to a supreme law or purpose, *i.e.*, in ethics.

Hence also the familiar distinctions between political and moral law:—(1) Morality is more *authoritative* than law, conscience than political institutions. Morality judges the latter, declaring them to be bad or good. A bad political law or institution is unfortunately a common phenomenon; a bad moral law is a contradiction in terms.* (2) Morality extends over a *wider field* than legal enactment. It takes account of all conduct, not of some departments only. This follows from the distinction already drawn between politics and ethics. For as politics is the science of the external conditions of morality, the corresponding art—practical government —takes account only of those kinds of conduct which endanger these conditions. These conditions are not indeed confined, as a popular philosophical dogma represents, to protection of person and property,—such a limitation is purely arbitrary,—they embrace family life, education, recreation, and everything that admits of public organisation in the interest of morality. Yet the details of conduct within the circle of these conditions, *e.g.*, within the family, the school, the theatre, lie outside this field, if for no other reason than their infinite

---

* The practical steps that ought to be taken in consequence of such an unfavourable judgment upon any particular law or institution will, of course, depend upon circumstances. The obvious formula in a country like our own is: agitation for reform *plus* temporary conformity. If any one thinks he can best agitate by refusing to conform, and taking the consequences, he may be admired for his moral zeal, but he will be punished for his political disobedience. The justification will be that more moral harm would come from leaving the law unvindicated than from punishing an enthusiast for reform.

multiplicity. (3) A deeper difference is that political law has to do with conduct in its *external consequences*, or if it goes deeper merely takes account of *intention*. It takes account of such visible effects as theft of property, neglect of wife and children, etc. On the other hand, the invisible things of the mind are recognised by most civilised governments as outside of their sphere. Morality regulates the *inward motive* * and disposition as well as the outward effect,—the conduct of the understanding and the imagination as well as conduct towards property or children. It says not only "Thou shalt not steal," "Thou shalt not kill," but "Think no evil," "Flee vain and foolish imaginations." This also follows from the distinction between the external conditions and the life for which these are intended to make room. Political enactment can maintain property, the currency, the family, public education; it cannot secure that the citizens shall use these institutions in the spirit and for the purpose for which they were intended,—a truth which is expressed in the common saying that you can not make men moral by act of parliament. The justification for legislation which apparently has this aim—*e.g.*, the regulation or suppression of public houses—is not that by means of it we may make certan persons conform to moral demands, *e.g.*, abstain from intoxicating liquor, but that we may improve the conditions of the moral life for the community at large, *e.g.*, for the neighbours or the children of the toper. The man who abstains merely because owing to the state of the law he cannot get liquor is obviously not moral. A distinguished churchman is said to have remarked to the late Professor Thorold Rogers, "We must have compulsory religion, because

* On the difference between intention and motive, see below, p. 58.

otherwise we shall have none at all," to which the
Professor replied that he didn't see the difference. The
same might be said of compulsory morality: it is equivalent to no morality at all. The further definition of
conduct, which, as we have just seen, is in its fullest
extent the subject of moral judgment, will be the object
of our next inquiry.*

* On the general subject of the relation between Law and
Morality, see Sidgwick's *Methods of Ethics*, Book I., ch. ii. ; also
Elements of Politics, ch. xiii. ; and on the apparent *permanency* of
the legal as compared with the moral code, Alexander, *op. cit.*, p. 286.

BOOK II

MORAL JUDGMENT

CHAPTER I

§ 14. What is Conduct?

WE have seen that ethics has to do with conduct and character, and that it differs from a physical or experimental treatment of the phenomena of human action in that its subject-matter is a form of judgment upon them. Before proceeding further we must try to get a clear idea of what is meant by conduct and character.

It seems natural to define conduct as "human action." And this is a good definition if we understand properly what is meant by "human action." For instance, breathing is a human action, but this is clearly not included in conduct, for we do not distinguish a good and a bad in automatic actions of this kind. In other words, the action is not distinctively human at all. It belongs to man as an animated mechanism, not as man. Nor do we mend matters by adding "conscious" to action, and identifying conduct with conscious action. I am conscious of winking my eyes when the sun strikes them, and of starting when I hear a sharp sound, but these actions are not yet conduct. They are known in psychology as reflex actions.* As such they are

* On the distinction between reflex action, instinct, and volition, see Höffding, *Psychology*, Eng. Tr., ch. vii., and for a full discussion of the " instinctive germs of volition," Bain's *Senses and Intellect*, pp. 246 full.

shared in by the lower animals, and are not distinctively human. The element that is still wanting is will or volition. Between the merely reflex and the voluntary action which constitutes conduct there is all the difference that there is (to take our previous example) between the blinking of the cat in the sunshine and the movement of my pen across this sheet of paper. The difference is that the latter is willed, so that we may define conduct as voluntary action.*

§ 15. Apparent Exceptions to this Definition

Against the view that moral judgment attaches only to voluntary action, it might be urged that we pass moral judgments on many actions that are not voluntary, *e.g.*, on habitual actions. How is this to be explained if moral predicates attach only to conduct, and conduct is always voluntary action? The answer is, that though the habit may have become so strong as to have completely mastered the will, and we can no longer be said to be responsible for its consequences, yet there was a time when each repetition of the action was voluntary. So that, while we cannot strictly be said to be responsible for the habitual act as an isolated event, seeing that it is not a voluntary one, we are responsible for it as an instance of a habit which has been voluntarily acquired, and which we ought to have checked before it became inveterate.† In other words, what we really judge in such a case is the series of voluntary acts whereby the habit has become irresistible. Contrariwise, if conduct and voluntary action are to

---

* On the distinction here drawn between conduct and action, see Lotze's *Practical Philosophy*, pp. 23 foll.

† See Aristotle's *Ethics*, Book III., ch. vii., where this point is raised, and once for all solved in the above sense.

be taken as equivalent terms, the difficulty might be raised that many actions are clearly seen to be voluntary, and yet are not commonly reckoned as conduct or made the subject of moral judgment. Thus it is thought that while the artisan is at his work, though all his acts may be strictly voluntary, yet they are not conduct: conduct (that in virtue of which we apply moral attributes to him) only begins when he lays down his tools. We do indeed blame him for being dilatory or careless in his work, but this is thought to be on the ground of his breaking his contract with his employer, not on the ground of the work itself. Similarly, in the higher fields of the artist and the scientific reasoner or experimentalist, we do not generally think of their labour as conduct. The distinction, however, here urged is entirely arbitrary, and cannot bear investigation. The conduct of the hand and eye and intellect in daily work is as much moral conduct as the voluntary dealings with ourselves and others outside that work. An artisan or an artist or a writer who does not "do his best" is not only an inferior workman, but a bad man.* Conduct then embraces not merely a section of man's voluntary life; it is not "three-fourths of life," as Matthew Arnold said of it, or any other vulgar fraction of it, but the whole of life so far as it is human life at all.

§ 16.   What is Will?

It remains to ask what this Will or Volition is which brings human action within the reach of moral judgment. The investigation of the phenomena of will as

---

* Carlyle once said of a joiner who was doing a job in his house in Chelsea that he "broke the whole decalogue with every stroke of his hammer."

a side or aspect of the human mind is one for psychology rather than ethics. Here it must suffice to give a short statement of the results reached by psychology, so far as they are necessary for the right understanding of what follows.

This will best be done by taking a simple instance and analysing it. Let us take the voluntary action of rising and going nearer to the fire. What does this involve? (1) Let us say it involves a feeling of pain arising from the sensation of being cold. *Feeling* is an element in all conscious action, and by feeling is meant simply pleasure or pain. This is involved even in the most unemotional actions, as in the investigation of a scientific problem. If there were no element of feeling, of pleasure in the thought of the acquisition of knowledge or of pain in the thought of being without it (*i.e.*, unless we had an *interest* in it), the activity itself would be impossible. In the case chosen for illustration it is obvious enough that there is an element of feeling, and that on the supposition that the action we have under analysis is voluntary this feeling makes itself felt distinctly as mine. It involves the incipient judgment, "I feel cold." In proportion as this is realised my state is recognised as different from the state of the cat which at the same moment shows signs of moving to the fire also. (2) There is *desire* of the warmth of the fire. It is important to note the new elements that are here introduced. (*a*) There is the idea of the fire and its heat in a particular direction and at a particular distance, and of myself as warmed by it. (*b*) Side by side, and contrasted with this, there is the idea of my present cold self, the contrast producing a heightened state of feeling curiously compounded of the pain of the present

state and the pleasure or interest in the idea of the
fire. (c) But if these two were all,—if the rise of the
idea of the fire were immediately followed by its enjoyment, as putting on the wishing-cap in the story means
possession of the thing wished for,—there would be no
such thing as desire or will. It is the fact that there is
resistance to be overcome, something to be done, that
is the condition of both. Desire is a state of tension
created by the contrast between the present state of the
self and the idea of a future state not yet realised. But
desire is not will, as may be seen from the fact that there
may be a conflict of desires in the mind, as, in our illustration, the conflict between the desire of getting on with
my work and the desire of getting up and going to the
fire. (3) This is the stage of *deliberation*,*_in which the
mind weighs, as in a balance, two or more mutually
exclusive objects of desire. Finally, Will, or Volition,
is the act by which attention is concentrated on the one
object of desire, to the exclusion of the others. Hence
there is further involved (4) the "*act of choice*," "deci-
sion," or "resolution," the essence of which is that I
identify myself in anticipation with a particular object
and with the particular line of action required to realise it. It may be, however, that the actual realisation
is deferred to a future time, *e.g.*, till I have finished
a book or a letter. In this case I am said to have
made a resolution, which means that the idea is, as it
were, hung up meantime in a state of suspended anima-
tion, to be called into life again when the proper moment
shall arrive. We do indeed pass moral judgments upon

---

* With reference to the object or end. At a later stage, after the
resolution has been taken, there is usually a subsidiary process of
deliberation as to the means.

resolutions,* but they are only provisional. A man is
not good because he makes good resolutions, nor bad
because he makes bad ones. It is only when the resolution passes into conduct that it justly becomes the object
of a moral judgment.†

§ 17. Relation of Desire to Will and Character

The chief difficulty in considering an act of will does
not, however, attach to the analysis of it into its elements,
but to the question of the manner in which we are to
conceive of these elements as related to one another in
the concrete act.

* And even on desires. See Matthew's Gospel, v. 28.

† How far the resolution is from the completed act has become
a proverb in respect to *good* resolutions It is not, perhaps, very
creditable to human nature that a similar reflection with regard to
bad resolutions does not make us more charitable to persons who are
caught apparently on the way to a crime. Höffding (*Psychology*,
Eng. Ed., p. 342) quotes a case of a woman who, having got into
a neighbour's garden for the purpose of setting fire to her house, and
been taken almost in the act, swore solemnly in court that she knew
she would not have perpetrated the act, but hesitated to state upon
oath that she had abandoned her intention when she was surprised.
With this we may compare the passage in Mark Rutherford's story
of *Miriam's Schooling*, where, speaking of Miriam's temptation to
take her own life, he says: "Afterwards the thought that she had
been close to suicide was for months a new terror to her. She was
unaware that *the distance between us and dreadful crimes is much
greater often than it appears to be.*" On the other hand, the mere
wish for a result (*e.g.*, Tito Melema's wish for his father's death in
Romola) may contain already in itself, all unknown to the conceiver
of it, the fully formed resolution and the act as well. The occasion only is wanting for the wish and the deed to spring together.
On the subject of the whole section, see Ward's art. on "Psychology" in *Enc Brit.*, p. 74; Green's *Proleg. to Ethics*, Book II.,
ch. ii.; Dewey's *Psychology*, pp. 360 foll.

Thus it is a common mistake to think of a desire as an isolated element. We speak of our " having desires," "following our desires," "controlling our desires," etc., as though they were something separate from ourselves, acting upon us from without, or controlled by us as an unruly horse is by its rider.* This conception of the relation between will and desire is at the basis of the anti-libertarian doctrine, that conduct is at all times determined by the strongest desire, *i.e.* (since desire is a force outside and independent of the will), by something other than free choice. The conception, however, is itself inaccurate. It is forgotten that desires are always for objects, and that these objects are always relative to a self for whom they have value. It is owing to their having a value for self that they become objects of desire, and thus their character, even their very existence, is always dependent upon the character of the self to whom they are objects. Thus it is an object of desire to the reader to apprehend this section on the nature of conduct, but it is so in virtue of his intellectual and moral needs, acquirements, and capacities. In other words, the desire depends upon, and is organically related to, the character of the person who desires to understand this book. This section has a significance and an attraction for him which it does not possess for the man in the street, precisely in virtue of the difference of their respective characters. His character reflects itself in the object of his desire; he thinks he sees, in the idea of himself as having read the book, a more desirable self than his present self: whereas to the man in the street the sight of the book and the paragraph

* See Plato's well-known simile of the charioteer and the horses, *Phædrus*, § 253.

gives back no such reflection, and awakens, consequently, no such desire.

These considerations bring out two points which are of the utmost importance in the theory of desire. First, human desires are not mere irrational forces or tendencies propelling a man this way and that way. They are always for objects more or less definitely conceived. As such they are to be distinguished from mere appetites or propensities which are shared by the lower animals. Secondly, these objects are related to a self, and that in two ways. (*a*) They are organically related, as just explained, to the character of that self. So far from being the creature of desire, each man may be said to create his own desires, in the sense that, as he himself changes by development of his intellectual and moral powers, he changes the character of the objects which interest him or which he desires. (*b*) They are related to the self, in that it is the realisation of them *for a self* that is desired. Hence it is indifferent whether we say, *e.g.*, I desire that object, or I desire myself to be in possession of that object: I desire to read this book, or I desire a self that has read this book. The essential point to note is that all desire, and therefore all will (inasmuch as will depends upon desire), carry with them a reference to self. Their object is a form of self-satisfaction.*

§ 18. Will and Self

The mistake of conceiving of will and desire as controlling or controlled from without is connected with the

---

* *Cp.* Bradley's, *Ethical Studies*, p. 62, " In desire what is desired must in all cases be self."

more fundamental one of conceiving of the will and the self as externally related to one another. As the former may be said to be the characteristic fallacy of those who oppose the common doctrine of the freedom of the will, the latter may be said to be the characteristic mistake of those who support it.* The latter often speak as though the self had, among its other faculties, also a will, which was free in the sense of being able to act independently of desire, and of the character which, as we have seen, reflects itself in desire. If what we have already said be true, we shall suspect this view, on the ground that, as we have already seen, will is dependent on desire, and all desire is related to self and character. We cannot be too careful to avoid thinking of the will as *possessed* by the self in the above sense. The will *is* the self. It is the self apprehended as consciously moving towards the realisation of an object of desire. It thus differs from conduct as the inward does from the outward aspect of the same fact. Looked at from the inside, the fact apprehended is that of a self expressing itself in conscious action with a purpose; looked at from the outside, it is conduct. Hence it will be indifferent whether we say that moral judgments attach to conduct or to the will (or self) that realises itself in conduct.

* It is not possible, perhaps not desirable, to enter, in a text-book like the present, into a full discussion of the vexed and difficult question of the freedom of the will. The above remarks are rather warnings against initial errors in approaching the subject than a detailed solution of its difficulties. For a critical discussion of the points at issue between Libertarians and Determinists, see Sidgwick's *Methods of Ethics*, Book I., ch. v.; and for development of a view similar to that in the text, Green's *Prolegomena*, Book II., ch. ii.

§ 19. Conduct and Character

In defining the subject-matter of ethics, we said that it was conduct and character; but hitherto we have not been in a position to set these two in their proper relations to one another. We have now, however, reached a point of view from which we may criticise the common ideas of that relationship. For these ideas are founded upon an error similar to those which we have just been criticising. They assume that the will, of which conduct, as we have just seen, is only the outer side, stands to the character in a merely external relation; the only difference being that, while by some it is conceived of as determined by it as by a natural cause (*e.g.*, as the motion of the billiard ball is determined by the cue), by others the will is conceived of as capable of acting in an independent line of its own, without relation to character. It will help us to steer our way between the rocks and shoals of this controversy, which will be recognised by the student as that between Necessarianism and Libertarianism, if we keep clearly before us two distinctions often overlooked.

In the first place, there is the distinction between the so-called natural tendencies and inherited characteristics, such as quick temper or indolent disposition, which are the raw material of moral training, and these same as elaborated and systematised by will and intelligence in that peculiar mode which we call character. The former, as isolated elements of character, may in a sense be said to be "given," and to be independent of will; though, as a matter of fact, they never come before us in a being whose conduct may be made the object of moral judgment, except in a form which they owe to the reaction of will and intelligence upon them. Character, on the other hand, is the acquired habit of regulating these tendencies in a certain manner, in relation to consciously conceived ends. In other words, character is not something separate from will and acting upon it from without, but is the habitual mode in which will regulates that system of impulses and desires which, looked at subjectively, is the field of its exercise.*

Secondly, there is the distinction between character as relatively fixed and static at the moment of action, and character as something that grows and changes from moment to moment.

In its former aspect volition must be conceived of as determined by character; the individual act must be taken as the expression or embodiment of character. If it be not so taken it is difficult to see in what sense we can speak in ordinary language of a man as responsible or accountable for his actions. The theoretic justification of moral responsibility is the presumption that a man's voluntary actions may be taken as an index to the moral qualities of the man himself. Any other hypothesis as to the relation between character and conduct—whether it be that of the determinist, who supposes actions to flow from previous conditions, as physical effects follow upon their causes, or that of the libertarian, who isolates the will from character as a mysterious power of unmotived choice—is incompatible with human responsibility. On the former hypothesis a human action is only one of a series of natural effects, for which it would be as absurd to hold the agent

---

* Hence character has been defined as a "habit of will." J. S. Mill calls character "a completely fashioned will."

accountable as it would be to hold the sun accountable for heat or the clouds for rain. On the latter supposition acts of choice are traced to an abstract force or entity, conceived of as without organic relation to the concrete self or personality who alone can be the subject of moral censure or approval.*

On the other hand, looked at as in process of formation or growth, character must be conceived of as determined by volition. As already pointed out,† our habits of conduct are the result of an indefinite multitude of past actions, which in the first instance were voluntary. If any one objects to this account, whereby he is asked to conceive of character as at once determining and determined by the will, we shall best answer by pointing out that this apparent contradiction is not peculiar to the relation of character and the individual act: it is simply a law of growth generally. The life of a plant furnishes us with an analogous instance. At any moment of its growth the plant is determined by its previous state; while, on the other hand, the new shoot (which corresponds to the volitional act) reacts upon and changes, or, in other words, determines, the future growth of the parent plant. We must, however, remember that, while in the plant the determining and the determined are unconscious of themselves as such, man (and herein lies his freedom) is conscious of himself as at once determining and determined by his character.‡

---

* On the subject of responsibility, see, *inter alia*, Bradley, *op. cit.*, Essay I.; Dewey, *Outlines of Ethics*, p. 160.

† § 15 and n.

‡ For discussion of the sense in which character can be taken as fixed, see Bradley, *op. cit.*, Essay I., Note B.

§ 20. Is Motive or Consequent the Essential Element in Conduct as the Object of Moral Judgment?

There still remains a serious difficulty in connection with the above account of the object of moral judgment. The object of moral judgment, it has been said, is conduct; but conduct, according to our definition, has two aspects: it is will and it is action; it involves an internal and an external factor.   On the one hand, as will it involves feeling, and desire, which again involves the idea of an object.   On the other hand, actions obviously involve consequences: in action the will goes, so to speak, out of itself, implicates itself in an external world, and in realising its object produces an *effect*.   Hence the question rises, Which of these factors is the important one?   Is conduct judged to be good or bad in respect of the feelings and desires involved in the volition, or in respect to the consequences which are involved in the action?   The controversy has become historic, some philosophers maintaining that the rightness or wrongness of an action depends upon the *motive*, others on the consequences.   On the one hand J. S. Mill asserts, "The motive has nothing to do with the morality of the act."   On the other his opponents maintain that "the rightness or wrongness of an act depends very much upon the motive for which it is done."

The question cannot be fully answered at this stage of our investigation.   The answer to it clearly depends in part upon our conclusions as to the kind of consequences which we shall agree to call good, *i.e.*, upon the answer we give to the question, What is the "standard" of moral judgment? which will be the subject discussed in future chapters.   Meantime it may be observed that much of the difficulty turns on the ambiguity of the word motive, upon which, in its relation to conduct, we are now in a position to throw some light.

§ 21. Meaning of Motive

It will be generally agreed that the motive is that which *moves* the will. It may therefore be looked for in one or other of the conditions which we found on analysis are implied in any act of will. These conditions are chiefly two, feeling and desire. In which of these are we to look for motive? (1) Some have said in feeling, and there is a sense in which it must be admitted that feeling is the moving spring of action. It is certain that there is no action which is not preceded by feeling. This is involved in saying, as we did, that feeling is invariably present as an element in desire. The pleasure-seeker must have a feeling of pleasure in the thought of a future pleasure before he can be moved to pursue it. Similarly the benevolent man must feel pleasure in the thought of other people's happiness, the scientific man in the thought of the truth to be discovered, before the will of either can be set in motion. But it is clear that this feeling cannot be the motive of an action in the sense required. For whatever else a motive is, it is agreed by all that it is equivalent to an end or aim representing something that is to be realised, *e.g.*, a future pleasure to ourselves, a good to others, or a truth to be discovered, not something that is already realised, as is the feeling in question. This may be otherwise expressed by saying that, while feeling as an element in desire may be said to be the efficient cause of action, a motive is universally admitted to be a final cause. Moreover, it is to be observed in connection with the question placed at the head of the preceding section that feeling, in the sense just explained, has in itself and as feeling no moral qualities whatsoever. It is only in virtue of its connection with certain objects that it acquires such a quality. Thus the feeling of pleasure in the thought of a pleasure is as a feeling neither good nor bad. Its moral quality depends wholly on the kind of pleasure which is thought of. Similarly the feeling of pleasure at the thought of a particular act of well-doing or a particular scientific investigation has upon its own right no moral superiority over any other feeling. It only derives its right to moral approbation from the object which kindles it; in other words, from the end or aim towards which the desire of which it is an element is directed.* (2) May we then look for the motive in the desire? It is clear that it cannot be *simply* the desire. Desire itself is said to be "moved," and, as we have seen, it is moved by the idea of an object; it is, in fact, that projection of the feeling self towards an object not yet attained which is the condition of volition. (3) Is then this idea of the object the real motive of the action? In a sense it is, but a question might still be asked, Is this idea of a desired object a motive *before* the will has chosen it, or only after the will has identified itself with the object and been "moved" by it? By some motive has been

---

* It might be said (Martineau seems to say so, *Types of Ethical Theory*, Part II., Book II., ch. vi., § 1) that malevolence is a feeling which is unconditionally bad. But malevolence is more than a feeling. It is, as the word indicates, a "*desire* for evil" to another. On the whole subject of the relation between feeling and motive, see Dewey, *op. cit.*, pp. 5, 6, 7, 10, 108. Also below, p. 110, and the words there cited.

taken, in the former sense, to mean the idea of any object presented to the mind as desirable. Popular language would seem to sanction this usage when it speaks of "a conflict of motives," as though several ideas were fighting for mastery. But seeing that the motive is that which moves, and the will is not moved until it chooses, it seems more correct to define motive finally as the *idea of the object which, through congruity with the character of the self, moves the will.**

§ 22. Motive and Intention

Further to clear the ground of preliminary difficulties which beset the question of the relation of motive and consequent to one another and to moral judgment, we must clearly distinguish between motive and intention. Bentham formulated this distinction by defining motive as that for the sake of which an action is done; whereas the intention includes both that for the sake of which, and that in spite of which, anything is done. Intention is thus wider than motive. The former may be said to include the latter, but not *vice versa*. For while the end or consequent for the sake of which the action is done is, of course, intended, it is only part of the intention, and is sometimes distinguished from the other part as the "ultimate intention." On the other hand, the consequences of the intermediate steps or the means adopted, though part of the intention, are not part of the motive. Thus the father who punishes his child is said to intend the child's good. The good of the child is the motive. But he also intends to cause the child

---

* On the subject of motive, see Green. *op. cit.*, Book II., ch. i., pp. 90 foll.

pain; the pain, however, though it is part of the intention, cannot in any sense be called the motive or reason
why he punished him. Or take the case of the man
who sells his coat to buy a loaf of bread. His motive
is to buy the bread. It is also part of his intention to
do so. It is part of his intention also to part with his
coat, but this cannot in any intelligible sense be said to
be the motive of his conduct.

§ 23. Bearing of Results on Question between Motive and Consequent

If we now revert to the question with which we started,
we perceive that the antithesis upon which the controversy turns is in reality a false one. Motive and
consequent are not really opposed to one another in
the manner supposed. The motive is the ultimate consequent as apprehended and willed. It is accordingly
indifferent whether we say that the motive or the consequent is the object of moral judgment, so long as
we understand what we are speaking about. Thus we
may say that an act is good because the motive is
good, but we shall be careful to note that by motive
we mean, not a mere feeling, but the end with which
the will identifies itself in the action, and by so doing
reveals its character. On the other hand, we may say
that it is the consequences which give moral character
to the act; but again we shall be careful to note that
this is true only if by consequences we mean, first,
consequences as preconceived, *i.e.*, as intended, and,
secondly, those of the intended consequences for the sake
of which the act is done, *i.e.*, the idea of which is the
final cause of the act. A man cannot be held respon-

sible for consequences which he did not foresee, except in so far as he is responsible for not foreseeing them. Nor is he to be judged good or bad on the ground of that part of the consequences which was his intention merely and not his motive. So judged, the regicide for the cause of freedom would be condemned, the tyrant who saved a victim from drowning to burn him at the stake would be justified. Only when we have taken into account the act as a whole, and answered the questions (1) whether the consequences as a whole are good or bad, (2) whether these consequences were the end aimed at, have we a right to found our moral judgments upon them.*

§ 24. Will and Motive

As a further consequence of our definition of motive, it will be seen that what was said in a previous section on the relation between will and desire applies, *mutatis*

---

* It has been said that most of the great historic controversies have turned on the ambiguity of words. The present seems an instance in point. Mill properly points out in his discussion of the above question (*Utilitarianism*, ch. ii. *n.*), that there is a distinction between *motive* and *intention*. He denies, however, that the motive has anything to do with the morality of the action, although he admits that the intention has. But on looking closer we find that he means by intention "what the agent *wills to do*," which, taken in the narrower sense of the ultimate intention explained, is precisely what we have seen to be the proper meaning of motive. From this he distinguishes motive as "the feeling which makes him will so to do," which is precisely what we have said motive ought not to mean, for the feeling, as feeling, has no moral quality whatsoever. Mill's opponents (*e.g.*, Martineau, see *Types of Ethical Theory*, p. 274) use the words in the same sense as he does. For the further discussion of the question raised in the text, and of other difficulties that rise out of it, see Green, *op. cit.*, Book IV., ch. i. init.

mutandis, to the relation between will and motive. Since
motive is the idea of the wider object desired, and since
the object desired depends upon the character of the
self that desires, the same may be said of the motive.
This is sometimes expressed by saying that a man "constitutes" his own motive. And this is true in the sense
that the motive is not to be conceived of as external
to the will, or as something that acts upon or appeals
to it from without. The mind and will of a man are
already expressed in his motives, so that in being determined by them he is in strict sense determined by himself.
Hence we may pass from judgment on a man's conduct
and character to judgment upon his motive, for in doing
so we do not pass from judgment upon will to judgment
upon something foreign to it. In judging a man's motive
to be bad, we pass condemnation on the character or
habit of will for being such that this could be a motive
to it.

§ 25. Summary

Returning from the discussion of these difficulties, we
may sum up the conclusions arrived at in this chapter, so
far as they are important for our main investigation. The
object of moral judgment is Conduct, *i.e.* voluntary action.
The Volition, or act of Will, which is the distinctive mark
of conduct, may be defined as the movement of the Self
towards the realisation of an object, conceived of, as a state
of its own being, as well-being or as good. Judgment
on conduct may therefore, with equal justice, be said
to be judgment upon will, or upon the self which is
expressed in the act of will. As, moreover, Character,
properly understood, is simply the general habit of will
determining it in its particular actions, moral judgments

attach with equal propriety to character. Finally, the Motive of an action is not, as commonly supposed, the feeling (which, though undoubtedly present in every act of will, has as feeling no moral quality), but the idea of the object in which the self is moved to look for satisfaction. Hence, as organically related to the self (being, in fact, only possible as a motive to a self of such and such a character), the motive is also with justice regarded as a proper object of Moral Judgment.

CHAPTER II

THE STANDARD OF MORAL JUDGMENT—MORAL LAW

§ 26. The Two General Forms of Moral Judgment

IF, in seeking for the standard of moral judgment, we start with an analysis of its form, we perceive at once that this is two-fold. On the one hand we speak of conduct as "right" or "wrong," and on the other as "good" or "bad." And these two forms seem to imply different standards. Looked at from the side of its etymology, right is connected with Lat. *rectus* = "straight" or "according to *rule.*" Similarly the word in Greek most nearly corresponding to right, Δίκη (Dikē), with the adj. δίκαιος (dikaios) and the adv. δίκην (dikēn = in early Greek simply "according to rule "), is connected with the root *dic*, to point or direct. On the other hand, good, Germ. *gut*, is connected with the root *gath*, found in Gr. ἀγαθός (agathos), and meaning serviceable or valuable for an *end.*

Similarly we have a circle of words referring to the phenomena of the moral life, and bearing obvious affinity to one or other of these fundamental ideas. On the one hand we have the vocabulary of right: *e.g.*, "duty," that which is owed or which we are bound to do;

"obligation," that which binds us; "ought," or owed; "responsibility," or answerableness, as before a legal tribunal, etc. On the other hand we have the vocabulary of goodness or fitness for an end: *e.g.*, in "virtue," the quality of fitness in a *man*, corresponding to Gr. ἀρετή (aretê), from root *ar*, found in ἀραρίσκω (ararisćô), to fit or join together; "worth," or value for an end, etc.

§ 27. Which of these is Prior?

There thus seem to be two standards, or at any rate two different ways of conceiving of the same standard, that of a law and that of an end; and the question may be raised, Which of these is prior, and what is their relation to one another? The answer is that while the conception of end, as we shall hereafter see, is prior in importance, being that on which the other rests, yet the conception of law comes first in time. Whether we look at the individual or the nation, we find that the earliest idea of morality is of a species of conduct which is imposed upon us by a law.* Thus each of us, at his first introduction into the world, finds himself in the presence of a law which he is conscious he did not make, and which seems to require from him an uncon-

---

* This, of course, does not prevent us from admitting that at the outset moral and political laws must have been recognised as serving some social utility. *Cp.* Green's *Prolegomena to Ethics,* Book III., ch. iii.: "There is an idea which equally underlies the conception both of moral duty and of legal right; which is prior, so to speak, to the distinction between them; which must have been at work in the minds of men before they could be capable of recognising any kind of action as one that *ought* to be done. . . . This is the idea of a common good." This is true even of religious practices. Their claim to respect must in the first instance have been

ditional obedience. The same is true of nations. The first idea of morality is of obedience to law. Nor is this idea confined to the primitive stages in a nation's development. Probably the prevalent idea among the vast majority of the inhabitants of civilised countries, at the present day, is that morality consists in doing what is right, or what is in accordance with a law laid down for human guidance by a Superior Will. Now while, as we shall see, there is a sense in which morality consists in obedience to an authoritative law, yet our first step must be to examine this popular notion as an account of the ultimate nature of the standard of moral judgment.

§ 28.   Three Stages in Reflective Analysis

In doing so we shall find that there are three clearly marked stages of reflective analysis, representing respectively the degree in which the human mind, in reflecting upon the contents of morality, has been able to rest satisfied with this primitive conception. (1) In more primitive times, and among individuals at a later stage of development who have not outgrown primitive notions, the law is conceived of as external. (2) At a later period, when reflection has shown this notion to be untenable, it is sought to supplement the defects of the

their serviceableness. *Cp.* Sir Alfred Lyall's *Asiatic Studies*, p. 56: "It will almost always be found that they [religious practices] are really founded upon some selfish material interests, and are not, as they are usually supposed to be, merely whimsical superstitions as to what will please the gods or as to what is right and proper." But it remains true that this origin is very soon forgotten: the law becomes, as it were, fossilised, and, resisting the forces that might have adapted it to new circumstances, is handed down as an unchangeable system of divinely given commandments.

traditional code, and to free the individual from bondage to an external authority, by appealing to the internal law of conscience. (3) While at a later stage still these two forms of "legal" morality come to be recognised by reflection as unable to bear the light of criticism, and give way to a new conception altogether, whereby the law is seen to be related to an end, which as intrinsically good and desirable determines ultimately our judgments of good and bad, and through them of right and wrong. We cannot do better, at this stage in our analysis, than avail ourselves of the help afforded by observing the course which, as a matter of fact, man's reflections on the nature and contents of the moral law have tended to take.

§ 29. (1) Morality as Obedience to External Law

The defects revealed by reflection, when it comes to react upon merely traditional codes which are conceived of as "given," are chiefly these : —

(*a*) Such codes are found to contain elements which, though they are commonly regarded as of co-ordinate authority, are clearly of unequal importance. Thus ceremonial are bound up with moral injunctions, moral and religious with political. A notable example of the former confusion and its subsequent correction is to be found in the history of the Jews. The burdensome ceremonial legislation which had been insisted upon by the traditionalist as of equal importance and sustained by the same authority as the moral* begins in the time of Amos and Hosea,† through the force of altered cir-

---

* An interesting survival is to be found in our own time in the Fourth Commandment.

† See Amos v. 21 foll.; viii. 5 foll.; Hosea vi. 6.

cumstances and a higher and more reflective moral feeling, to be recognised as a matter of quite secondary
importance, if not entirely irrelevant, to morality.   In
the teaching of the New Testament, as is well known,
the ceremonial has dropped entirely away.   As an example of the way in which political duties may come to
be recognised as distinct from and subordinate to moral
and religious duties, we have the Greek drama of *Antigone*.
Its interest to the moral philosopher * lies in the fact that
it marks the recognition by the writer, and the Athenian
people whom he addresses, of the inadequacy of a merely
traditional and aphoristic code to meet the varied
demands of the moral life.   In individual life it is unnecessary to illustrate the distress which the conflict
between a moral command and political or paternal
authority frequently creates in persons to whom moral
duty has been presented solely or chiefly in the form of a
system of external rules.

(*b*) But the conflict is not confined to elements so
obviously distinct as the ceremonial or political and the
moral.   Within the laws recognised as moral, contradictions necessarily rise.   The commandment "Thou shalt
not steal " may come into conflict with the commandment
"Thou shalt do no murder," † "Thou shalt not lie " with
"Thou shalt do no injury to a fellow-creature."   The
practical needs of life are sufficient to reveal this defect
in traditional morality, though conscious reflection
is not slow to follow and emphasise the unconscious
criticism of changing circumstances.   Thus the industrial changes in Athens had already sapped the

---

* See Caird's *Hegel* (Blackwood), p. 6; Jebb's *Antigone*, Introd.,
p. xxi.
† See Plato's *Republic*, § 331 and whole passage.

traditional code, before the criticism of the sophists came to assist and accelerate its disintegration.

There are two ways in which the would-be conservators of a traditional code may, under these circumstances, endeavour to meet the difficulty. They may try to stretch the code so as to make it co-extensive with life. In other words, by inventing a system of explanations and exceptions they may attempt the impossible task of making their code cover every possible case. This is the *reductio ad absurdum* of the notion that morality can consist in obedience to an external law. It was the mode adopted by the clergy of the middle ages in reference to the ecclesiastical code. It resulted in the development of that system of Casuistry which has fallen into such deserved disrepute. Another way is to seek for one chief commandment among many lesser ones.* Thus the doubts and difficulties of the faithful were settled in the Christian Church by advancing the doctrine of Passive Obedience, according to which the supreme duty was implicitly to accept the decisions of king and pontiff as the oracles of God. The demand for such a commandment springs from a truer instinct,—

---

* On a celebrated occasion when the question, "Which is the great commandment?" was raised, the misunderstanding it involved was shown by the selection in reply of one that could not by its very nature be a commandment at all, being a direction to *feel*, not to act. In reality the answer went beyond the idea of law, and substituted for it a *principle* of action. It expressed this principle in subjective terms of feeling (love), but other passages show that it was conceived also in terms of an objective end. It was "the Kingdom of God" which "is within you." The distinction between Rule and Rational End corresponds to that between "the Law" and "the Gospel," between the ten words and the good word or the word about the Good.

the instinct, namely, to seek a principle of unity which will introduce order and subordination into the multiplicity of the traditional code. So far it is right. It is wrong in that the principle that is sought is still an external one. It unifies by suppressing and destroying, not by co-ordinating and vitalising the parts. In this way the doctrine just referred to meant in this country the suppression of the inward witness of conscience against untruth and injustice in favour of the duty of obedience to the powers that be. Or, to take another example, the golden rule that we should love our neighbour as ourselves has been referred to in the above note as a principle of conduct rather than a commandment. But it has frequently been interpreted by devout Christians in the latter sense, and in this case it obviously leaves room for conflict and contradiction between its terms. Thus I have heard it seriously argued that it only commands us to love our neighbour *as* ourselves, the implication being that when, as often happens, a conflict arises between our own and our neighbour's advantage, we require a further guide. The answer which is merely authoritative is in favour of one side or the other, and settles the dispute by making an arbitrary selection of one of two apparently contradictory maxims. The discovery, on the other hand, of a principle which will mediate between them, and give each its place in an organic system of duties, is the problem of rational ethics.

(*c*) A further difficulty is raised by reflection upon the nature of the moral life itself. If, as appears according to the view we are considering, this consists in obedience to a law which is merely "given," it does not require much insight to see that, however august the authority upon which it rests,* this authority itself can only be grounded on a *force majeure*. In other words, the interest which man takes in it can only be an indirect one, having been made artificially to attach to it by means of threatened punishments and promised rewards. But what is this but the destruction of morality itself? For whatever else morality may be, it is universally acknowledged by all who reflect upon it to be something more than slavish submission to a superior will on the ground of its superior power.

§ 30.　(2) The Law as Internal—Conscience

These difficulties it has been sought to meet by representing the standard of moral judgment under another form. The law, it has been said, that constrains us in the field of conduct is not really the external law at all, or this only in so far as it finds a response in the inner law of conscience. It is this inner law that is the authoritative court of appeal. The external law may contain irrelevant matter, and enjoin at times contradictory lines of conduct; but we are not left without an inward witness and guide, that is sufficient for all emergencies, and is the ultimate standard and test of moral judgments.

We must therefore examine, in the second place, the claim of conscience to be ultimate and supreme. And first we shall have to ask more particularly what is here meant by conscience.

By conscience is here meant the intuitive faculty of

* To the Greek, Themis (Law) was the daughter of Uranos (Heaven). The Jews, as is well known, traced their moral code to the legislation of Sinai.

moral judgment, with the characteristic feeling that
accompanies its exercise. (*a*) It is claimed that it
is intuitive, *i.e.*, it does not arrive at its results through
any process of reasoning, but acts immediately. Acts
of fraud and cowardice are condemned instinctively;
acts of truthfulness, courage, temperance, are as instinctively approved. (*b*) It is said to be underived. It
cannot be analysed into simpler elements, being an
ultimate fact of human nature. Hence the peculiar
authority of its judgments, which command our allegiance
irrespective of all secondary considerations, such as
interest or pleasure. (*c*) It is universal. It is found
among all races, the lowest as well as the highest,
and among all ages and classes. By this it is not, of
course, meant that it is found among these in an equally
developed form, any more than is the faculty of dis-
criminating colours, or of reasoning; but that whatever
development the faculty may or may not subsequently
undergo, it is innate in just the same sense as are the
faculties of sight and hearing, and just as universal as
these are in all normally constituted human beings.

§ 31. Mistaken Objection to Intuitionalist View

In criticising this, which is known as the Intuitionalist
view of the standard of moral judgment, it is important
not to mistake our ground. Thus we must put aside as
irrelevant an argument that is frequently brought against
it, viz., that the judgments of conscience do not possess
that easily recognisable character which this theory
attributes to them. They may easily be mistaken, it is
argued, for various less dignified judgments and feelings.
Thus conscience is frequently not distinguishable from

mere sense of propriety, reverence for custom, or fear of committing an offence against etiquette.* But this does not seem to be true. An appeal to consciousness seems to reveal a clearly distinguishable line of demarcation between the two phenomena, failure to distinguish which is as much a matter of intellectual as of moral obtuseness.†

There are, however, insurmountable difficulties in accepting this theory as a final account of the standard of moral judgment, and these I must now proceed to state. As a preliminary it is necessary to go a step further than I have hitherto done in the analysis of conscience.

§ 32. Elements in Conscience

It is clear, when we reflect upon it, that conscience involves at least two distinguishable elements. (*a*) There is an intellectual element. Conscience is a faculty of *judgment*. Nor is this judgment merely logical. It is not merely a judgment of fact. It is also judicial. It is a judgment upon fact. This judicial attitude of conscience is a prominent characteristic of it. Conscience in its

---

* "You ride using another man's season ticket, or you tell a white lie, or speak an unkind word, and conscience, if a little used to such things, never winces. But you bow to the wrong man in the street, or you mispronounce a word, or you tip over a glass of water, and then you agonise about your shortcoming all day long; yes, from time to time for weeks. Such an impartial judge is the feeling of what you ought to have done."—Royce's *Religious Aspect of Philosophy*, pp. 53, 54.

† The case, of course, of survivals such as that mentioned p. 74 *n.*, in which what has come to be a mere convention is still *mistaken for* a moral obligation, is different.

usual manifestations seems to be engaged in a species of judicial investigation. Older writers delighted in this metaphor, which they worked out to show that, as common language seems to imply, conscience is at once lawgiver, accuser, witness, and judge. Conscience, it is said, "commands," conscience "accuses," conscience "bears witness," conscience "acquits" or "condemns." They might have added, as we shall immediately see, that it is also executioner, seeing that it punishes with "stings" peculiar to it. So prominent is this element of judgment, that by some it has been held to be its chief or only one. It is thought to be in a peculiar sense the voice of reason, and has been elevated into the position of a special faculty, which under the name of the moral faculty, or the faculty of moral judgment, had a prominent place assigned to it in the older text-books. (*b*) It is clear, however, that this is not the only element, or perhaps the most distinctive. It is as involving a characteristic *feeling* that the judgments of conscience come most home to us. This is especially marked, as is to be expected, in judgments upon past conduct,—the feeling of remorse, as is well known, being one of the most violent of human emotions. Hence some writers have gone to the opposite extreme from those who would exclude feeling altogether, and claimed for conscience that it is wholly a matter of emotion.* This view seems to gain some support from popular language, which substitutes "moral sentiment" and "moral feeling" for conscience, and endows them

---

* "The approbation of praise and blame cannot," says Hume (*Inquiry concerning Principles of Morals*, § 1), "be the work of judgment, but of the heart, and is not a speculative proposition or affirmation, but an active feeling or sentiment." *Cp.* Professor Knight's *Hume*, B., ch. vi. (Blackwood).

with all the judicial attributes which we have seen to
belong to the latter. That this view involves the inaccurate use of language is obvious, inasmuch as feeling
may emphasise and, in the metaphorical sense referred
to above, give effect to the judgments of conscience, but
as feeling it is dumb and cannot pronounce them.
Nevertheless the side of the phenomena of conscience
which is here emphasised is a true and important one.*

§ 33. Defects of Conscience as Ultimate Standard

(*a*) *The elements of feeling and judgment may stand
in contradiction to one another.* Returning once more to
the criticism of the Intuitionalist theory, we may state
the first difficulty thus: So long as the two elements
of conscience just described are in harmony with one
another,—so long, that is, as the appropriate feeling
accompanies the intellectual approval or condemnation
of an act,—little practical difficulty may arise in the
conduct of life. But suppose, as is frequently the case,
that reason approves of a line of conduct which yet, on
being chosen, is accompanied by a feeling bearing a close
resemblance to remorse. How are we to explain such
a conflict? and which of the conflicting elements must
we follow? † Psychologically, the explanation is simple
enough. It is that feeling is the conservative element

---

* On the general subject of conscience, see below, pp. 220 foll.,
and authorities there cited.

† The reader will supply instances for himself. The contradiction
between reason and feeling which some of us will recollect, when
first we permitted ourselves to take a row or attend a concert on
Sunday, is a good example from contemporary life.

in human life. In the present case it continues to attach
to certain lines of conduct in the form of remorse, or, as
we say, "qualms" of conscience, even after reason, the
radical and revolutionary element in life, has pronounced
in their favour as morally innocent.* The ethical question, however, still remains, Which of these elements has
the more authoritative claim upon us? Whatever our
answer to this may be (whether we take our stand upon
the instinctive feeling, or upon the rational judgment),
we shall have to go further, and seek for a reason for
our preference in the ultimate nature of conscience, *i.e.*,
we shall have to seek a standard of judgment as between
the elements of conscience itself.

(*b*) *Relativity of judgments*. But secondly, within the
field of the element of conscience which we described
as judgment, serious difficulties present themselves.
What, it may be asked, are these judgments? The
common answer is, that they represent the generally
recognised principles of right and wrong: as that lying,
cheating, unchastity are to be reprobated; truthfulness,
honesty, temperance are subjects of approbation. In
other words, it is the "middle axioms" † which are
intuitively discerned. But if this is so, what becomes
of the universality which we saw above is claimed on
behalf of the judgments of conscience? Instead of the
universal agreement on the main lines of moral obligation which the theory demands, we find a perfect chaos

---

* Another instance is the feeling that continues to keep us attached
to institutions after we know them to be useless, or to individuals
after they have ceased to merit our regard.

† What Aristotle calls the major premise of the practical syllo-
gism: All lying is wrong; the completed argument being this would
be a lie, therefore this is wrong.

of contradictory principles at various times and in various places,* and the standard of right and wrong is still to seek.

If it be sought to meet this difficulty by giving a different answer to our question, and maintaining with some that "though undoubtedly men differ in different ages and countries as to what they judge to be right and wrong, yet they are all agreed as to the fact that there is a right and a wrong, and this is what is declared to be innate," this is to give up the whole position. For it amounts to the assertion that we know intuitively that there *is* a standard, but that intuition is helpless to tell us what the standard is.

If, finally, it be said that what is intuitively apprehended is not right and wrong as such, but the true end of human life, we have passed to a new theory altogether. We have passed from the theory that the standard of moral judgment is ultimately to be conceived of as a Law, and we have substituted for it a theory of the End. In this form Intuitionalism can no longer maintain itself as an independent theory. For whatever end we suppose thus to be intuitively revealed, the task of ethics is still before us, viz., to show that moral judgments do not rest on a number of isolated intuitions, but are organically related to an end or good. On the other hand, on any theory of the end, we may very well admit that its worthiness is intuitively discerned, in the sense that it is the necessary postulate of morality, and is not in the last resort susceptible of other proof.

(*c*) *The authority of the law still external.* In discussing

* See the classical proof that there are "no innate practical principles."—Locke's *Essay concerning Human Understanding*, Book I., ch. iii., and Book V., ch. ii., below.

the conception of morality as obedience to external law, we saw that difficulties rose, not only from the demand forced upon us, both practically and theoretically, to find some principle of unity in the particular injunctions of which it consists, but also from the consideration of the nature of its authority. If the law is merely external, it can only be recognised by man in virtue of its sanctions, that is, the pains and penalties which are decreed by another as the price of disobedience; and this was seen to be the destruction of morality, and the substitution for it of a long-sighted prudence. To meet this objection it was suggested that the law is not merely external, but is the voice of conscience. This led us into some account of conscience, with the result that its injunctions have been seen to lie just as much outside one another as those of external law, and therefore leave us with our explanation or principle of unity still to seek.

We have now, therefore, to ask, in the third place, with reference to the authority of the law on the intuitional theory, whether it has really been made internal by being called the law of conscience? To be "internal" in the sense demanded, the law must be seen to be really *our own*, not merely the law of some *part* of us. If it is the law of a part only, it is still external to the self, and obedience to it on the part of the self is, after all, obedience to something which is external. Our question, therefore, resolves itself into this: Is conscience, on this theory, the name for the whole self, judging and feeling in a particular way, or is it only a part, connected indeed with the self in that it inhabits the same body, yet to all intents and purposes a stranger there?

Now our final objection to the theory that we must

rest content in ethics with the intuitions of conscience is that, as commonly maintained, *it leaves the law still external* in the sense just explained. Conscience is not explained, as on any true theory it must be, as the self judging of its own acts,* but (as the very phraseology of the intuitional theory implies) as a special faculty. It is the " Faculty of Moral Judgment,"—an innate and inexplicable power of moral discrimination, sitting apart from the rest of human consciousness, like the priestess in the oracle at Delphi, and authoritatively imposing its decrees upon the human will. The whole conception may easily be shown in psychology† to be contrary to the teaching of science; it is now seen to contradict the presupposition implied in the whole vocabulary of moral praise and blame, viz., that morality is free obedience to a self-imposed law.

§ 34. (3) Morality as determined by End

It is indeed possible to correct this theory so as to meet the demand made upon it in the last paragraph. It may be said that conscience is the whole or true self claiming to legislate for the parts. Its claim is the claim of the self, as a conscious and rational being, to judge any particular manifestation of itself in voluntary action. Its voice is the voice of the true self, or of the self as a whole, which, as addressed to the false or partial self of particular desires and passions, rightfully assumes the tone of command, and has built up in connection with

---

* See below, p. 220.

† The human mind cannot be treated, as in the older text-books, as an aggregate of " faculties." The elements of mind, viz., feeling, thought, will, etc., are related to one another in a closer and more organic way than this mode of conceiving them represents.

the varied circumstances and desires of life that system of authoritative commandments known as the moral law. Morality consists in obeying this voice. Man's freedom just means his power of being moral, *i.e.*, of obeying the imperative of reason or of his true self. But, in making this correction, it is clear that we have passed beyond the conception of the standard as Law, and substituted in its place the idea of an End. There is indeed a moral *law* which is authoritative and supreme; but it is now seen to be so not by indefeasible right of its own, but in virtue of its relation to the true self, as the End which man, quâ man, seeks to realise.

The following books will be occupied with the further definition of the end which is the standard of moral judgment. Meantime we may conclude this part of the discussion by noting some of the general characteristics of this end, as these flow from the conclusions already reached, and may prove useful as tests both of current theories about it and of the view hereafter to be set forth.

§ 35. General Characteristics of the End *

(1) It is important to observe that we are dealing in ethics with a conscious being, to whom the end is a possible object of *desire*. Hence ethics is a teleological as opposed to empirical science. It deals with a final cause or consciously conceived purpose, not merely with an efficient cause or general tendency of *things*. Closely connected with ethics, and liable to be confused with it, there is the science of biological evolution, which shows

* The remaining portion of this chapter is not essential to the main argument, and may be here omitted by the student who desires to follow closely in its track.

how efficient causes have been at work in bringing human consciousness to the birth as the soil out of which morality springs. But it is a mistake to refuse, as is frequently done, to recognise that in passing from biology to ethics we are passing from an empirical to a teleological science. The mistake is made possible by the fact that there is a sense in which biology is also teleological, in that it deals with the tendency of organisms to adapt themselves to environment; and thus, through the law of natural selection, to develop forms of life which *we*, with a reference to the end of consciousness and social life, call higher. But there is an important difference between the end with which biology and the end with which ethics and politics deal; viz., that in the one case it is worked out by beings who are unconscious of it; in the other it is an end which is consciously conceived. To overlook this distinction, and to attempt to solve ethical problems by the methods of empirical science, is one of the chief causes of confusion in working out the doctrine of the end.

(2) That it is a good, and a *personal* good, follows from the fact that it is a consciously conceived end. As such it is an object of desire, and, as we have already seen, "object of desire" and "personal good" are equivalent terms.* This must not, of course, be taken to mean that the end is necessarily self-interest. We shall have abundant occasion hereafter to deal with this fallacy.† Meantime, it is sufficient to warn the student against confusing two totally different things, viz., personal good and personal advantage. Whatever the end may

---

* *Quidquid petitur petitur sub specie boni.*

† In addition to what will hereafter be said, see the excellent treatment, Dewey, *op. cit.*, § xxxv., and the authorities there cited.

be—whether happiness, or duty, or perfection—it can only become an object of choice to us in so far as it is recognised as desirable, *i.e.*, a personal good, or good for us. The difference between a selfish and unselfish theory of ethics is not that on the former the end is conceived as personal, on the latter as impersonal good, or as no good to the self at all. The difference lies in the account which they severally give of the nature and contents of the personal good.

(3) It further follows from the fact that, as has been shown above, it is the end of the self as a whole, that it is *intrinsically* good. It is good in *itself*, not as a means towards any further good. Other ends, such as health, wealth, learning, are goods of the self under particular aspects: as a physical being, as wealth-producing, truth-seeking, and hence are contributions or means to a further good. The end of man, as man, cannot contribute to anything higher.* Hence it cannot consist of anything which does not possess interest for man, as that in realising which he will find his personal good. It cannot, for instance, be mere obedience to the will of God. Such obedience cannot in itself be an object of interest or desire. Those who represent obedience to the will of God as the supreme duty do not suppose that it can. They tacitly assume that man's chief end is his own happiness, and that this will best be secured in this world and the next by the course of conduct they recommend. The view really undermines morality by substituting for it a long-sighted prudence. It is accordingly a true intuition which makes the higher moral feeling of the

---

* *Cp.* Aristotle's account of the end as self-sufficing (*Nic. Ethics*, I.).

Church now insist that the relation of God to man is
not that of a master imposing a law upon his servant,
but that of a father to his children: the essence of the
latter as opposed to the former being that a father
recognises that his claim upon the obedience of his
children rests upon the reasonableness of the law, as
enjoining conduct which is for their *good*.

(4) It is only stating the fact of its intrinsic goodness
in another way to say that the end is *summum bonum*.
But we must be careful not to mistake the meaning
of the expression.   It does not mean that the good
can be conceived of in any sense as a *sum* of particular
goods or satisfactions.   Human life does not consist
of a *number* of activities, each directed from moment
to moment towards the satisfaction of a separate desire.
It does not require much reflection to discover that our
daily life, so far as we are intelligent beings, does not
consist in the pursuit of a number of isolated equally
important ends, but is a *system of ends*, each of which
is more or less consciously subordinated to one beyond
it, until, in the case of a "consistent" life,* we finally
trace them all up to the aim, purpose, or final end of our
lives.   In a like sense, the good for self, as such, is not a
mere sum of isolated satisfactions, but is the final end in
reference to which all others have their place and value
assigned to them.

At the same time we have to avoid the mistake of
thinking of the good as though it were the satisfaction
of some supreme or highest principle distinct from and
tyrannising over the desires.   The supremacy which it

---

* On the other hand, one of the most charming characteristics
of children and of non-moral beings is that all their ends are
equally important.

exercises is not, so to speak, exercised in its own interest
as separate from the interests of the particular desires.
" Reason," says Aristotle, " rules the desires like a consti-
tutional statesman," *i.e.*, as their representative, and for
the good of the whole, not for its own good as having an
interest separate from theirs. In other words, the self is
not something different from human desires, with separate interests of its own, but is these desires organically
related to one another in a system or whole. It is, on
the one hand, made up of them, varying from moment
to moment as one or other of these is dominant; on the
other hand, it is the principle of unity which expresses
itself in them, dominating them and bringing them into
that unity which we call personality. It is nothing
apart from the desires and activities which it unifies:
these, on the other hand, would be mere blind instincts of
propensities apart from that principle or organic relation
through which they become a self. Hence the good of
the self or whole, while it is more than the good of any
of the particular parts or desires, cannot be secured,
except through the relative satisfaction of each of them.*

* The conception of the Summum Bonum as a harmony or equilibrium of the elements of human nature comes to us from Plato. It
may be contrasted, on the one hand, with the Hedonists' view, which
makes good consist in a *sum* of satisfactions, and, on the other, with
Kant's, which makes it consist in satisfying the demands of reason,
regardless of desire. Recently it has been worked out with much
skill by Mr. Alexander in the first part of his *Moral Order and
Progress*. It is, however, a mistake to suppose, as Mr. Alexander
seems to do, that mere formal equilibrium of function, apart from
the satisfaction of the self of which it is the condition, can ever of
itself be the end.

§ 36. These Characteristics of the Moral End the Basis of commonly recognised Attributes of the Moral Law

These characteristics of the end explain the peculiarities which are commonly recognised as distinctive of moral law. So long as we interpret moral judgment as merely a judgment of conformity to law, it is, as we have seen,* inexplicable. Hence we were forced to conclude that such judgments, while prior in time to those of value, as being the form under which we first make acquaintance with morality, are later in ethical importance. On the other hand, to depose the idea of moral law from its logical pre-eminence is not to cancel its practical claims; to explain the law by showing that its utterances have reference to an end, as the principle of unity which underlies them, is not to explain it away. On the contrary, it is to establish the law in possession of its traditional attributes, by showing the *reason* of its claim to them. Thus, in showing that the end is supreme, we have established the supremacy of the law of which in practice it is the source, as other ends (*e.g.*, correct reasoning) are the source of the practical maxims that flow from them (*e.g.*, the rules of logic). On the same ground we may claim that the law is absolute or "categorical." As the end is one which man, as man, is called upon to realise, it carries with it a law or maxim from which there is no escape, the law, namely, of which all other moral laws are only the

---

* Pp. 69, 70, where we saw that this interpretation involved us in contradictions, by requiring us to make morality a means to a further end.

particularised expression—"Be a man."*   Finally, we may claim to have established its dignity as a "law of liberty" by showing that it is not imposed from without, but flows from the conception of an end which is self-imposed and intrinsically good.†

* Hegel's well-known formula is, "Be a person," to which, as we shall hereafter see, "and respect others as persons" is a necessary addition.

† For the practical value of moral rules as "tools of analysis," see Dewey, *op. cit.*, pp. 203 foll.

BOOK III

THEORIES OF THE END

CHAPTER I

§ 37. Problem arising out of Results hitherto reached

RETURNING to the point we reached in examining the proposal to make conscience the ultimate standard of moral judgment, we may now state the problem which will occupy us in the immediately succeeding chapters.

We there found that the moral judgments implied in the utterances of conscience are only intelligible as the judgments of a self which, as the principle of unity among the particular desires, and more than any one of them, claims to sit in judgment upon them, and demands that they shall each and all give way when, as may frequently happen, their satisfaction is incompatible with its own. The Satisfaction or, as we provisionally expressed it, the Realisation of this Self is thus the end which is the standard of moral judgment.

If now we proceed to inquire more closely into the nature and definition of this end, it is at once obvious that our conclusions will depend upon the conception we entertain of the nature of the self which is to be satisfied or realised. For there are different elements in the self, and according to our view of the relation of these to one another will be our notion of the nature of the

89

self as a whole. Thus, there is an obvious distinction, which the earliest psychologists were not slow to note, between Thought and Feeling,—between the active powers of thought and reason on the one side, and the passive element of feeling which comes and goes with the varied experiences of the self on the other. A question, therefore, at once arose, traceable in the very dawn of philosophy, Which of these elements constitutes the true nature of the self? Is feeling the primary and essential element, reason having for its function in the last resort only to administer to the satisfaction of a feeling or emotional self? or is reason the vital constituent in its composition, while feeling is only a transient effect playing upon its surface? In accordance as one or other of these alternatives has been accepted, throughout the history of philosophy, is the view that has been taken of the ethical end. If the self is *par excellence* a feeling self, its *summum bonum*, it has been argued, must be a state of feeling; if it is *par excellence* reason, the end must be some form of rational activity.

The examination of these two historic theories will be of use in helping us to a truer one, by teaching us to benefit by the truth and avoid the mistakes of each.

The more important, because the more common, is the first, which will accordingly occupy the main portion of this, the critical part of our investigation. Stated in its simplest terms, it is the view that the end is the agreeable state of feeling which we call Pleasure.

§ 38. What is meant by saying that the Standard of Moral Judgment is Pleasure

By this theory in its simplest form it is meant that conduct has value in proportion to the amount of pleasure it produces. One line of conduct is good relatively to another which, when it is possible to produce less, produces more pleasure; that is bad which, it being possible to produce more, produces less pleasure.

There is no difference in motive, according to this theory,—all men being moved alike by the one motive, desire for pleasure. The difference is in the amount of pleasure which, owing to insight into the conditions of happiness and their previous moral training, their actions tend to secure. Thus, the intemperate man is reprehensible, not because he pursues his own pleasure,— we all not only do that, but we cannot do anything else, —but because he habitually chooses courses of action which involve to himself, his family, and to society at large, an amount of pain far exceeding the pleasure which the momentary indulgence gives to himself. When it is possible for him to create a balance of pleasure by restraining himself, he has done the reverse and created a balance of pain. Similarly the liar gains immediate pleasure or advantage,—so far his act is good,—but the pain and disadvantage ensuing to society, in increased suspicion, mutual distrust, impaired credit, etc., far outweigh the pleasure, and the conduct must accordingly be stamped as bad. The worst conduct is that which under the circumstances yields—or, since there are many counteracting circumstances, tends to yield—the least possible amount of happiness. That conduct, on the other hand, is best which tends to produce the greatest sum-total of pleasure.

§ 39. Ancient Forms of the Theory

This theory of the end, in a more or less fully
developed form, has, as is well known, played an important part in the history of ethical thought.   It
made its appearance in the early morning of philosophy.   The teaching of Socrates, whose influence,
like that of Christ, was rather due to his life and
character, than to any system of doctrine which he
propounded, contained a number of elements loosely
held together.   Upon his death these fell apart, as did
the different elements in Christian doctrine,* and were
taken up by different groups of his followers, and made
the basis of different theories of the end of life.   One of
these groups seized upon the element of feeling, and
under the name of the Cyrenaics † (from the city of
Cyrene, to which Aristippus, the chief exponent of the
doctrine, belonged), became the precursors of the later
and better-known school of Epicureans.   They held
that pleasure was the end, interpreting this to mean
the pleasure of the moment, and using the theory as
little more than an excuse for self-indulgence.

At a later time the theory was taken up by Epicurus, ‡
who deepened and dignified it (1) by connecting it with
the atomic theory of the nature and origin of matter
as expounded by Leucippus and Democritus, (2) supplementing it with a sensationalist psychology, and
(3) interpreting pleasure so as to include the higher
social and intellectual enjoyments.   The noble expres-

---

* *E.g.*, Faith and Works as represented respectively by Paul
and James, Universalism and Judaism by Paul and Peter.

† See Zeller's *Socrates and Socratic Schools.*

‡ See Cicero's *De Finibus*, Book I., c. 5-21 (Bohn's Library).

sion which was given to this theory of the nature of
the world and human life by the greatest of the Roman
poets, Lucretius,* is well known.

§ 40. The Theory in Modern Times

The doctrine has been revived in modern times chiefly
by English thinkers, who differ from their predecessors
in antiquity (1) in seeking to provide it with a securer
basis in philosophy and psychology, (2) in enjoining a
more reflective form of pleasure-seeking, (3) in making
the doctrine the starting-point for enlightened theories
of social and political reform.   The discussion of the
first of these differences belongs to a text-book of psychology rather than of ethics.   The development of the
theory in the direction indicated by the third difference
coincides generally with the successive appearance of
Egoistic, Universalistic, and Evolutionary Hedonism† to
be discussed below, and need not further detain us here.
The second, however, requires more detailed notice, as
it introduces us to a development which is characteristic
of the modern form of the theory, and will best find a
place at the point at which we have now arrived.

§ 41. The Sanctions of Morality

Ancient Epicureanism, while emphasising the peace
and happiness which have their source in the recognition
of the universality of natural law, laid but little stress on

---

* See *De Rerum Natura*, Eng. Tr. (Munro).

† For the name see below (p. 96). Besides the Bibliography,
p. 238, see, for the history of modern Hedonism, Courtney's
Constructive Ethics, Sidgwick's *History of Ethics*, and Sorley's
Ethics of Naturalism.

the physical consequences of conduct as a motive to morality. As the doctrine, moreover, was developed at a time when the older forms of pagan society were breaking up, and men were seeking satisfaction for their deeper longings in a species of spiritual individualism, it laid but little emphasis on social approval as a source of happiness, or social disapproval as a source of pain. Finally, as it was a fundamental article of the creed of the Epicurean that the gods, if there were any, took no interest in human affairs, and that man's life ended with the grave, it was impossible to appeal to the rewards and punishments of another life as a motive for good conduct in this. In modern times, however, the keener sense of the relation between cause and effect in the physical plane, the increased sensitiveness to public opinion resulting from greater social solidarity, together with the habits of thought encouraged by the common form of the Christian religion, suggest reasons for the conduct commonly called moral, which the supporters of Hedonism have not been slow to seize upon and develop. These reasons or persuasives to good conduct are the so-called "sanctions of morality," the enumeration of which is a characteristic addition to the modern form of the pleasure theory.

By the sanction of a *legal* enactment is meant the penalty that is annexed to the infringement of it. In ethics, as just explained, the meaning is extended to include the pleasures which are the persuasives to conformity, as well as the pains which act as deterrents from disobedience to moral law. The sanctions of morality in this sense are mainly five: (1) There is the natural sanction, by which are meant the physical pains which follow upon the disregard of natural laws, e.g., in the

over-indulgence of the appetites. (2) There is the
political sanction, or the pains and penalties attached by
law to such obviously "unfelicific" forms of conduct as
theft, assault, libel, etc., and the public rewards and
honours bestowed upon the social benefactor. (3)
There is the social sanction,—the pleasures of social respect, gratitude, etc., which a favourable public opinion
brings with it, and the pains of the disgrace attaching to forms of immoral conduct, which do not come
within the reach of the law as well as to those that do.
(4) There is the religious sanction. Though this does
not belong to the catalogue of legitimate motives on a
naturalistic theory of ethics like ordinary Hedonism, yet
in speaking of the sanctions or external persuasives to
morality founded on the desire for pleasure and aversion
to pain, it is necessary to take account of the influence
which fear of punishment and hope of reward in another
life have exercised, and still continue to exercise, in the
moral education of the race and the individual. (5)
To these is added, as a fifth, the moral sanction, by
which is meant simply the pleasures of a good conscience
and the pains of remorse.*

We shall have occasion hereafter to discuss at length
the presuppositions on which the whole theory is
founded. Meantime it is sufficient to point out that
to any but the Hedonist the phrase "sanctions of
morality" is suspiciously like a contradiction in terms.
Conduct which issues from regard for these sanctions is
not morality, if by that we mean conduct which is

---

* For the theory of the sanctions of morality, see Bentham's
Morals and Legislation, ch. iii.; Mill's *Utilitarianism*, ch. iii.;
Sidgwick's *Methods of Ethics*, Book II., ch. v.; Fowler's *Pro-
gressive Morality*, chs. i., ii.

morally approved. It may conform to a certain type
and be externally indistinguishable from good conduct,
but it is not *good*. The man who is temperate because
he desires the pleasures of temperance (whether these
be earthly or heavenly, physical or social) is, as Plato
pointed out, temperate by reason of a kind of intem-
perance. Similarly, the man who is courageous from
fear of the pains which will be the consequence of
cowardice is courageous by reason of a kind of cowardice.
Appeals to the so-called moral sanction, *i.e.*, to the
pleasures of a good conscience (or the pains of remorse),
as a motive to good conduct, appear, moreover, to
involve an additional absurdity. The pleasure in question depends upon the approval of conscience, and this
in turn depends on the disinterestedness of the conduct,
i.e., upon the exclusion of the idea of personal pleasure
from the motive. To point therefore to the pleasure
likely to result from such approval, as a reason for well-
doing, is to suggest a motive which, if accepted, would
render approval impossible.

§ 42. Pleasure and Happiness

Some confusion has been introduced into the discussion of this theory in the forms under which we now
know it by the failure to distinguish between pleasure
and happiness. Assuming that they both refer to a
state of agreeable feeling, it is not true, as is commonly
assumed, either that the terms are synonymous, or that,
if there is a distinction, happiness is only pleasure
raised to a higher power by an arithmetical process of
multiplication or addition.* The distinction between

* In thus becoming affiliated with pleasure, happiness seems,
like so many words, to have come down in the world. Certainly

them is founded on a qualitative difference in the
modes of self-realisation which pleasure and happiness
severally accompany, not merely on a quantitative
difference in the amount of the feeling itself. Pleasure
is the feeling which accompanies the satisfaction of particular desires; happiness is the feeling which accompanies the sense that, apart from the satisfaction of
momentary desires, and even in spite of the pain of
refusal or failure to satisfy them, the self as a whole
is being realised.* The propriety of describing the end
in terms of either depends upon the conclusion we shall
come to in the sequel as to the legitimacy of describing
it in terms of feeling at all. Meantime I may so far
anticipate as to point out, for the benefit of those who
may prove impervious to the arguments there adduced,
that there is less objection to expressing the good in
terms of happiness than in terms of pleasure pure and
simple. For while both descriptions of the end err in
identifying it with agreeable feeling, the happiness theory
(Eudaemonism) has the advantage over the pleasure
theory (Hedonism) that it refuses to consider the *summum bonum* as a mere aggregate of particular pleasures,
and insists that it is pleasure for the self as a whole.†

For the benefit, however, of those who are determined

the Greeks would have objected to the assumption which underlies
modern Hedonism, that pleasure and happiness are interchangeable
terms, or differ only as the less from the greater. To them ἡδονή
(hêdonê = pleasure) conveyed a wholly different idea from εὐδαιμονία
(eudaemonia = happiness), and accordingly Hedonism would have
represented a wholly different theory from Eudaemonism.

* On this distinction the student is recommended to consult
Dewey's *Psychology*, pp. 292-4.

† Which, as we can never insist too often, is more than a mere
aggregate of its parts.

at all hazards to express the end in terms of feeling, it
may be well to state that to advance a step further and
call it Blessedness, which, Carlyle says (*Sartor Resartus,*
Book II., ch. ix.), is better than happiness, is less misleading still. Blessedness may be defined as the feeling
of pleasure which accompanies modes of conduct in
which an existing harmony of activities is sacrificed to a
higher conception of what a true harmony implies, in
other words, in which the self as static is sacrificed to
the self as progressive. Seeing, therefore, that man, as
man, is a progressive animal, and that harmony is no
sooner established between himself and his environment
than it is broken into by aspirations after a higher form
of life, the theory which represents the emotional reaction of such aspirations and the activities resulting
from them as the end, while theoretically not less
erroneous than that which defines it in terms of any
lower form of feeling, may yet by reason of its implicit
admissions be less practically misleading.

§ 43. Do Pleasures differ in Quality?

A difficulty suggested by the discussion in the preceding paragraph has risen within the school itself as to
whether pleasures differ only in quantity, or in quality
as well. There are those who hold that pleasures differ
only as greater or less, and that, in estimating the comparative value of two or more lines of conduct, we have
only to cast up the arithmetical total of the pleasures
which they severally tend to produce. Others hold
that pleasures differ in quality as well. The controversy
carries us into psychology, in which field the answer is
seen to depend on considerations already set forth in a

previous section (21), where it was pointed out that it is impossible to consider feelings, quâ feelings, as qualitatively differing from one another.   It is only in virtue of the qualitative differences of the objects in connection with which they rise that we are justified in attributing moral quality to them.   Thus, on the hypothesis that knowledge is a higher good than wealth or power, the pleasure of acquiring it may be judged to be higher than that of gratified vanity or ambition.   But from the Hedonist's point of view knowledge can only be judged a higher end in so far as it is the source of a greater quantity of pleasure.   In other words, the qualitative differences in objects are reduced to quantitative differences in the feeling of pleasure they produce.   To introduce, therefore, into the pleasure theory qualitative differences among feelings which are not resolvable into quantitative, is to introduce a standard of *higher* or *lower* in a scale of relative dignity or worth not determinable in terms of greater and less.   It is to go beyond the conception of self as a subject of feeling, and to declare that there is another standard besides the greater or less agreeableness of its experiences, viz., their *worthiness* as experiences of a being who is more than feeling, and may have higher ends than pleasure.*

§ 44.   How are Pleasures calculated in respect to their Value?

For those Hedonists who hold the simpler and more logical view that pleasures differ only in respect to quantity the question still remains, What dimensions must

---

* On this controversy see Mill's statement of the doctrine that there are differences of quality among pleasures, *Utilitarianism*, p. 12 (10th ed., 1888), and the criticisms of it in Kant's *Theory of*

enter into the calculation? What elements enter into
the "pleasure calculus"? We calculate the size of a
room by the three dimensions of length, breadth, and
height. What are the dimensions of a pleasure? Jeremy Bentham was at pains to formulate them as six,—
intensity, duration, nearness, certainty, purity, fruitfulness.* With the exception of the two last these explain
themselves, and need not further detain us. The two
last, however, require a word of explanation. By purity
is meant not any moral quality, but freedom from
accompanying pain: an intellectual pleasure may in this
respect take precedence of a sensual, on the ground that
it does not involve subsequent pain, as the latter is liable
to do. By the fruitfulness of a pleasure is meant the tendency to bring other pleasures with it, as when keeping
an engagement involves the pleasures of a good conscience and the future benefits that might accrue to the
good character for reliableness which is thus acquired.†

§ 45. Modern Forms of the Pleasure Theory

Difficulties of a still more fundamental kind arise
when we ask the question, "Whose pleasure is meant?"
Differences on this head have given rise to at least two

Ethics (Abbott), p. 109 (4th ed.); Green, *op. cit.*, Book III., ch. i.,
§§ 162 foll.; Bradley, *op. cit.*, pp. 105 foll.; Dewey, *op. cit.*, pp. 46
foll. Also Alexander, *op. cit.*, pp. 203 foll.

* See *Morals and Legislation*, ch. iv. The seventh of the dimensions he enumerates, viz., extent, introduces a difficulty excluded
from this paragraph.

† The arithmetic of pleasure becomes more complicated when to
the pleasures of this world are added the pleasures of the next.
Thus Paley gave himself a longer sum by trying to combine the
pleasure theory with the orthodox Christianity of his time. His

different forms of Hedonism. Agreeing in the psychological doctrine that each not only does, but must,
pursue what at the time appears to be his own greatest
pleasure, supporters of the pleasure theory have still
differed as to the proper mode of formulating the end
which is the standard of moral action. (1) There are
those who maintain that the end of rational conduct is
no other than the pleasure of the individual himself.
Moral judgments are the judgments that are passed
upon conduct according as it is adapted to secure this
end in the highest degree possible for the individual,
or, through his ignorance or folly, fails to do so. This
section of the school is known as the Individualistic or
Egoistic Hedonists.* (2) There is Altruistic or Universalistic Hedonism,† which takes the pleasure of others
also into account. It is important to note the precise
point in which this differs from the former doctrine.
It does not differ in its account of what is ultimately
desirable. It agrees that this is pleasure. It merely
introduces a new element into the pleasure calculus. In
addition to the dimensions already mentioned, it enumerates the *extent* of the pleasure as the most important
consideration of all. This, it need hardly be pointed
out, makes a vital difference; for whereas upon the
former view his own pleasure counts to the individual as

naïve definition of virtue, as " doing good to mankind in obedience
to the will of God and for the sake of everlasting life," has been
wittily said to combine "the maximum of error in the minimum of
space."

    * Best represented in modern philosophy by Thomas Hobbes.

    † Represented in this country by William Godwin, Bentham,
James Mill, J. S. Mill, and Professor Sidgwick in various degrees
and in divers manners.

supreme, and that of others is only sought as tributary
thereto, according to the form of the theory now under
consideration, and familiar to every one under the more
popular name of Utilitarianism, the pretensions of the
individual sink into insignificance. "Every one is to
count for one, and no one for more than one." The
pleasure which is the standard of moral judgment is not
the greatest pleasure of the individual, but the "greatest
pleasure of the greatest number," calculated upon the
basis of the equality of the claims of all.*

§ 46. Characteristic Difficulties in these several Forms of Hedonism

(1) *Egoistic Hedonism.* A detailed criticism of the
pleasure theory in its two chief forms is beyond the
scope of the present handbook.† It must here be
sufficient to refer to characteristic difficulties which
attach to each.

The stumbling-block in the way of the Egoistic

---

* As has been well pointed out in Green's *Proleg. to Ethics,*
Book III., ch. iii., § 214, it is this democratic principle which has been
illogically added to the theory, and not its contention that the end
is pleasure, which has made utilitarianism so effective as a principle
of legislative reform, and, it may be added, so popular as a principle of individual conduct.

† Besides the authorities referred to (p. 238), the student will find
exhaustive discussion of the Hedonistic hypothesis in Green's
Proleg. to Ethics, Book III., chs. i. and iv.; Book IV., ch. iv.;
Alexander's *Moral Order and Progress,* pp. 196 foll.; J. S.
Mackenzie's *Introduction to Social Philosophy,* pp. 202, 226;
Dewey, *op. cit.,* pp. 17 foll.—where the important distinction is
made between "pleasure as the (only) object of desire" and
"pleasure as criterion" of moral value; Bradley's *Ethical Studies,*
Essays III. and VII.; Caird's *Critical Philosophy of Kant,* Vol. II.,
p. 229.

Hedonist, over which he has always tripped, and may
now be said to have fallen to rise no more, is the obvious
outrage which is committed against the moral sentiments
and benevolent impulses by the attempt to explain them
as modifications of the selfish desire for pleasure. The
attempt may be made to do so either directly, as by
Hobbes and his followers,* who sought to resolve altruistic
impulses, such as those of compassion and benevolence,
into reflex forms of personal fear or hope; or indirectly,
as by the later Hedonists,† who sought by means of the
principle of the Association of Ideas to explain how
virtue, which at first is pursued only on account of the personal pleasure or the exemption from pain which it se-
cures, may afterwards, by a confusion of means and end,
come to be pursued for its own sake. The difficulty of
explaining altruistic conduct upon this basis has led the
lineal descendants of this school to acknowledge, besides
the egoistic, the altruistic impulse of sympathy as a co-
ordinate principle of action.‡

(2) *Universalistic Hedonism.* Universalistic Hedonism,
or Utilitarianism, has had difficulties of its own to contend
with, the chief being to explain how, on the presupposition which it shares with the former view that his own
pleasure is the only object that any one can desire, it is

* " Self-love," says Larochefoucauld, " lingers with strange objects
only as the bees with the flowers, in order to draw from them what
it requires." Quoted by Höffding, *Outlines of Psychology*, Eng.
Tr., p. 244.

† *E.g.*, Hartley. See *Observations upon Man*, Part I., ch. iv., § 4.

‡ The attempt made by evolutionary writers to explain egoistic
and sympathetic feelings as developments from a common root (see,
e.g., Höffding, *op. cit.*, pp. 247 foll.) does not, of course, alter their
qualitative distinctness in their fully developed forms.

possible to desire the greatest happiness of the greatest
number. The difficulty did not much trouble Bentham,
the father of Utilitarianism, who airily explained the
phenomenon of his own undoubted benevolence, by saying that he was a selfish man, "whose selfishness hap-
pened to have taken the form of benevolence." In another passage he assigns their respective places to egoism
and altruism in the characteristic saying that "self-regard
alone will serve for diet, though sympathy is very
good for desert." His successor, J. S. Mill, found
this a tougher knot. He tried to solve it by the
famous argument in the fourth chapter of *Utilitarianism :*
"No reason can be given why the general happiness
is desirable, except that each person . . . desires his
own happiness. . . . Each person's happiness is a good
to that person, and the general happiness therefore
a good to the aggregate of all persons." This is as
though one were to argue (to borrow Carlyle's famous
comparison), that because each pig desires for himself
the greatest amount of a limited quantity of pigs'
wash, each necessarily desires the greatest quantity for
every other or for all.* Latter-day utilitarians, who are
naturally dissatisfied with such an argument, prefer to
renounce the dogma that personal pleasure is the one
thing desired, and so are free to maintain, as some do,†
that we ought to desire universal happiness because
Reason bids us. The ultimate desirableness of the
greatest general happiness is thus made to rest upon the
dictum of Reason. But what, we still ask, is Reason?
and why should I listen to her voice? The theory in

* Upon which ingenious mode of argument see any book on
logic under head "Fallacy of Composition."

† *E.g.*, Professor Sidgwick, *Methods of Ethics*, Book III., ch. xiii.

its present form leaves us with these questions un-
answered.*

§ 47.   Elements of Value in Pleasure Theory

While these objections seem fatal to the several forms
which the theory has taken, it ought not to be forgotten
that this view of the end has usually had to maintain itself
against equally one-sided theories, and is thus not without
value as a protest against their falsehood.   Thus it has
always been opposed to the theory, to be dealt with in the
next chapter, which invests mere resistance to desire with
peculiar merit, and which tends to emphasise the ascetic
or negative element in the moral life at the expense of
its positive side as a form, not of self-denial, but of self-
satisfaction or self-realisation.   Similarly, in the field of
law and politics, the service of the founders of utilitarianism at the beginning of the present century to legal
and political reform is inestimable.   It may indeed be
questioned† how far Bentham, Godwin, Place, Grote,
Austin, J. S. Mill, were inspired by the Hedonistic, as
opposed to what might be called the Democratic,
elements in their theory.   But it is certain that, at a time
when other theories by their conservatism and mysticism
seemed to favour the maintenance of established abuses,
the Hedonistic writers brought forward an apparently
simple and intelligible standard, by which the utility of
laws and institutions might be estimated.

---

* See the criticism of this view, Green's *Prolegomena to Ethics*,
Book IV., ch. iv., §§ 364 foll.; Bradley, *op. cit.*, pp. 114-117. The
answer to the question necessarily leads us to a conception of the
nature of the self as essentially *rational*. But this annihilates the
presupposition upon which the Hedonistic theory rests (see p. 90).

† See above, p. 102 *n*.

§ 48. Fundamental Error of the Theory based on inadequate Analysis of Desire

The error of the theory, in what has been called its "psychological," * which is also its logical form, consists in the relative functions which it assigns to reason and feeling in the moral life. The end which is the standard of value in conduct is supposed to be given immediately. It is the end, not only of man, but of all sentient creation. "All sentient beings," it is said, "desire pleasure by a law of their nature." The difference between rational and non-rational beings lies not in the character of the object of desire, but in the relative degree in which they possess the capacity for its enjoyment and apprehend the means of its attainment. Similarly, among beings nominally rational, differences consist in the relative perception which they have of the means whereby the greatest sum-total of pleasure may be realised. In other words, the function of reason is that of directing and regulating action in view of an end which is immediately given by feeling. Reason gives no end: it merely prescribes the means to the attainment of one which, on appearing upon the stage, it finds already universal and inevitable. Accordingly, the rationality or value of conduct has to be judged, not by the character of its end or object, but by its suitability as a means

---

* The form which it takes in more recent writers (see p. 104 fin.) I regard as transitional, and as likely to be merged either in evolutionary hedonism or in the view set forth in these pages. It is chiefly important at the present time as having received the support of so great an authority as Professor Sidgwick.

towards the realisation of that which alone has value, viz., agreeable consciousness or pleasure.

In all this there is a fundamental misconception as to the relation of thought or reason to desire, which our analysis of the latter has already furnished us with the means of correcting. We have already seen that the *idea* of the object (in the example we employed, the idea of warmth), as affording satisfaction to the self, was an essential element in all that is properly called desire. This means that reason does not simply *accept* the object given it by a natural impulse or propensity, and set about devising means for its realisation. It would be truer to say that it makes the object, inasmuch as there can be no object of desire without it.

Comparing this conclusion with the view under consideration, we see (1) that an "object of desire" can only exist for a being which thinks and reasons as well as feels, and that it is an abuse of language to say, as the Hedonist has done from time immemorial,* that all sentient beings desire pleasure. (2) The rationality or value of conduct for us as human cannot, it is now seen, be measured by the extent to which it tends to realise an object given irrespective of reason. The question is, how far an object which, *ex hypothesi*, is a state of feeling, can satisfy a being who has just been shown to be more than feeling. Merely to put this question suggests a suspicion of the unsatisfactoriness of the Hedonistic answer. We saw at the outset that this theory was based upon the assumption that the self was primarily and essentially Feeling. When this is shown to be groundless; when, in the mental phenomenon with which we have in ethics primarily to deal, viz., human

---

* See Aristotle's *Ethics*, Book X., ch. ii.

desire, it is seen that a self is at work which is more than
feeling, we may reasonably doubt whether the end, which
is the standard of the judgments of value we pass upon
human conduct, can be a form of feeling. If, as we
were previously led to believe, the end is the realisation
of the self as a whole, and if, as we now see, this self is
more than feeling, it is impossible to hold that it can
obtain the satisfaction which it demands in what is
admittedly a mere form of feeling.

§ 49. Is Pleasure the only Motive? Re-statement of Hedonistic Argument

The above argument, however, may be acquiesced in
without shaking the reader's conviction that pleasure is
the only motive of action. Thus after taking the utmost pains to make the above objections plain, I have
frequently been met with the following reply: "All you
say may be very true, but you fail to convince me that
it is possible for me to act from any other motive than
desire for my own pleasure. Even when I flatter myself
that I have at last succeeded in performing a really
self-denying and disinterested action, closer inspection
invariably reveals to me that I have only done it because
I pleased, or because it pleased me so to do. Even
extreme cases of so-called self-sacrifice—as, for instance,
that of the martyr—are seen on further scrutiny to be
only subtler or more eccentric forms of self-pleasing. It
is not necessary to maintain that, in such a case, the
object is any form of sensuous pleasure, either in this
world or the next. All that is argued is, that the course
of action which the martyr chooses must, in some way
incomprehensible to ordinary mortals, have pleased him
—is in fact only his eccentric way of 'enjoying himself.'

In this respect saint and sinner, martyr and pleasure-seeker, are alike: the only reason each can ultimately give for preferring one form of life to another is, that it gives him greater pleasure."

Now we might meet this objection, as it is sometimes proposed to do, by merely pointing out that it rests on an ambiguity in the English word "please." "It pleases me to do a thing" may mean either "It gives me pleasure to do it," or simply "I choose to do it." This distinction * may be clearly indicated by translating these phrases into their corresponding Latin equivalents, *amœnum est* and *placet*, which give respectively the noun-adjectives *amœna* = things that give pleasure, and *placita* = things chosen or resolved upon. Now if in the above contention the word "please" is used in the latter sense; if in saying that I always do what I please, or what pleases me, I simply mean I always act because I choose to act, the statement cannot indeed be said to be false; it is only meaningless. It is equivalent to saying, I always choose because I choose. With all the appearance of assigning a reason, the sentence assigns no reason at all. If, on the other hand, it be meant that I always act because the action will please me, or because of the pleasure it will give, the statement is comprehensible indeed, but it is precisely that against which the batteries of our argument have in the last few sections been directed.

But this mode of meeting the objection only leads my opponent to a more careful statement of it. "It is obvious, of course," he will say, "that the statements 'It will give me pleasure' and 'I choose' have come to be regarded as different, but the point of my contention

* On which see Sidgwick, *op. cit.*, Book I., ch. iv.

just is that this is a superficial distinction. On a closer
scrutiny, 'to choose' is seen to be the same thing as 'to
find pleasure in,' which in turn merely means 'to hope for
pleasure from.' Or, putting choice aside—as being only
determination by the strongest desire, *i.e.* (according
to my interpretation), by the greatest pleasure, where
several courses present themselves—and confining ourselves to desire, what I contend is, that to find the
idea of a thing pleasant, and to desire it, are one and
the same, and that to say so is merely another way
of saying that the only object of desire is pleasure."

§ 50. Met by Distinction between "Pleasure in Idea" and "Idea of Pleasure"

To meet this form of the objection, it is necessary
to look more closely than we have hitherto done at
the relation of pleasure to desire. In treating on a
previous occasion of the phenomenon of desire, we
touched on the relation to it of feeling in general. We
saw that feeling enters into it as one of its constituent
elements. Thus there is in all desire a feeling of pain
in being without the object of desire. It is now necessary to observe that besides this pain, and contrasted
with it, there is the pleasure which the idea of the object
(another of the constituent elements in desire) gives
us. This pleasure is known in ordinary language as
"interest"—"the interest which the object excites."
Strictly defined, it is the feeling of the value which the
object has for the self.*

---

* Mr. Bradley defines pleasure generally as "the feeling of self-
realisedness" or "affirmative self-feeling" (*Ethical Studies*, p. 234).
As an element in desire, it might be defined as the feeling of
anticipated self-realisedness, or the feeling of the congruity of the
object with the natural wants or habits of the self.

Now it may be admitted that there is a sense in which this feeling may be said to move to action.* We may even go further, and admit for argument's sake that the idea of the course of action chosen, *e.g.*, by the martyr, gives him greater pleasure than the idea of any other possible course. But to make this admission is one thing, to contend that in choosing that course he chooses his own pleasure, or is moved by the desire for pleasure, is quite another. Indeed the one contention is exclusive of the other. If the pleasure that moves us be excited by the idea of an act, it cannot at one and the same moment be excited by the idea of a pleasure. The idea of pleasure of course may move us, but then the pleasure becomes an object of desire, and must in turn excite a present pleasure. It follows then that the pleasure which moves (if it be pleasure which moves) cannot be the pleasure aimed at; nor is the contention that we are always moved by the pleasure of the idea before the mind equivalent to maintaining that there can be no motive save desire for pleasure.

To pursue the question further, and to ask in what sense we can be said to be moved by the pleasure of the idea, and whether it is true that we are always moved to action by the idea which excites the greatest pleasure, would lead me too far from my present subject. Enough has been said to show the groundlessness of the Hedonistic contention, either in the form that pleasure is the end, or that it is the only possible motive to action.

* See p. 56 above.

CHAPTER II

THE END AS SELF-SACRIFICE

§ 51. Opposite Theory to foregoing   ˙

In the last chapter I examined the theory which is
founded on the conception of the self as primarily
and essentially a subject of feeling, animated by the
one prevailing desire of securing the greatest satisfaction to such a subject, *i.e.*, the greatest sum-total
of pleasure.   In this chapter I proceed to consider
a theory which in many respects stands in direct
antithesis to it.   It is founded on the view that the
predominating element in the self is reason, which,
as essentially opposed to desire, asserts itself in the
authoritative and categorical demands of the moral
imperative.   On this theory the end of man as a rational
being is unconditional obedience to this imperative, as
the law of his inner being or true self.   Pleasure, so far
from being the end, cannot enter into our conception of
the end of action without vitiating any claim which it
may otherwise have to be considered virtuous.   In order
to be good an act must be done out of reverence for the
reason which enjoins it, and without respect to the consequences.   As opposed to the theory that the end is

pleasure for pleasure's sake, this theory has aptly been called the theory of duty for duty's sake.*

§ 52. Historical Forms of Theory

This theory has taken various forms, reappearing from age to age, and gaining importance from its antagonism to the rival view. Thus, when the Socratic circle broke up into what are known as the minor Socratic schools, and the Cyrenaics asserted the doctrine that the end was to seize the pleasure of the moment, they were opposed by the Cynics,† who taught that, on the contrary, pleasure was an evil, and that the true good consisted in independence of all forms of passion or desire. At a later date the Stoics proved themselves superior to their Cynic precursors in presenting a more dignified view of human personality, and in the emphasis they laid upon the active life; but they were in fundamental agreement with them in holding the chief good to be life in accordance with reason, by which was meant the life in which passion and desire played the smallest, reason, or, as they expressed it, "nature," the largest part. Under like influences the ascetic elements in Christian morality were developed. It was as a protest against the easy-going naturalism of pagan morality that the exaggerations of hermits and anchorites, and later the whole monastic system, had their value. In our own century the current Hedonism has found its corrective, since the time of Kant, in the theory set forth in so

---

* See the admirable contrast between these two views in Bradley's *Ethical Studies*, Essays III. and IV. See also Dewey, *op. cit.*, pp. 78 foll.

† The school is represented in popular thought by Diogenes, who, however, had little to do with developing its fundamental tenets.

notable a form * by that philosopher, viz., that the only absolutely good thing is the Good Will, which has been interpreted to mean will determined by reverence for reason as revealed in the moral law and untainted by any lower motive.†

§ 53. The Theory recognises Right as distinct from Expediency

It must be recognised at the outset that this theory is not open to the objection which common-sense morality has always brought against Hedonism, that it confounds the distinction between what is right and what is prudent. On the contrary, the theory before us stretches the distinction to the point of denying any relation between them. Opposed to the desires, which by their very nature are self-seeking, it is held that there is another principle of action which is radically distinct from and may determine us independently of them. The suggestions of desire may doubtless conflict with one another, and reason, in the sense of reflection, may be called upon to arbitrate between them. This regulation of conflicting desires in such a manner as to secure the sum-total of selfish advantage is known as prudence. But desire, as a whole, is maintained to be by its very nature in never-ceasing conflict with reason as such, and virtue consists in denying altogether the claim of the former to determine the action of the rational will. Right thus stands out clear

* See Kant's *Theory of Ethics* (Abbott).

† Corresponding to this philosophical theory we have, in ordinary life, the test which many well-intentioned, but usually somewhat ineffective persons, habitually apply to their conduct as a test of the purity of their motives, " Am I doing this because I like to, or because it is right?" the assumption being that one cannot like what is right and be all the better for doing so.

from the taint of all prudential considerations. Let these once enter into the motive of an act and its claim to moral rectitude is destroyed.

With this qualitative difference between prudence and morality is connected the absoluteness with which ordinary moral consciousness invests the moral law. So long as the so-called *summum bonum* only differs in quantity from the particular goods which are the object of particular desires, it is difficult to see where an "ought," *i.e.*, an absolute or categorical imperative, can come in. The end in reference to which such an imperative has meaning must be a universal one, *i.e.*, one which it is reasonable to demand that all should pursue. It cannot be conditional on their "liking to." Now it is quite true that the Hedonist represents the greatest pleasure as a universal end, but then the form which the greatest pleasure takes to each individual is by its very nature particular. Granted that the so-called "middle-axioms" of morality, "Thou shalt not steal," "Thou shalt not kill," etc., are generalisations from experience as to the mode best fitted on the average for realising this end, they have authority for the individual only on the hypothesis that there are no other modes, and that his idea of the greatest pleasure is the idea of the average man. Obedience to them can never be required unconditionally.* "You *ought* to do this" can have no meaning, as an unconditional command, to the consistent Hedonist. The rejoinder, "Yes, *provided* I recognise that action as a means to my greatest pleasure; but I don't," puts an end to the matter. But on the theory under discussion

---

* Hence the tendency of the older Hedonist writers to represent the middle axioms as the invention of government. Virtue is "the interest of the stronger."

it is different. Reason is the same for all. Being, moreover, that which is distinctive of man, it speaks in the name of his true or permanent self, as opposed to the transient phases of appetite and passion which he shares with the lower animals. Its law accordingly is the law of liberty. To disobey reason is to renounce man's special birthright of freedom,—the freedom that consists in submitting to a self-given law, and refusing to be enslaved by the alien authority of a merely natural inclination. It is not therefore open to the individual to plead the peculiarities of his sentient nature in excuse for disregarding the imperatives of reason. These are binding upon him as a rational being. To deny their authority is to deny himself part or lot in the kingdom of humanity.

§ 54. Value of this View of Man's Nature in the History of Thought

It is in virtue of this uncompromising attitude towards the lower life of desire that this theory, and the view of life founded upon it (in spite of their one-sidedness), have exercised so important an influence upon thought and life.

The theory that the essential element in man, or that to which he is called upon to give effect, is his reason, has usually risen into prominence in the history of civilised nations at periods when, owing to external misfortunes or the decay of national institutions, the world has offered little that could satisfy man's higher aspirations. This was notably so at the time of the rise of the Stoic philosophy, when, owing to the decay of free national life among the Greeks, the individual found himself thrown back upon the resources of his own inner life for support to the sense of human dignity and freedom which could no longer be found in civil and political life. It was even more conspicuously so during the early ages of the Roman Empire, when, in a rich and highly cultured society, "all men were slaves but one." To have kept alive under such circumstances the heroic view of life, as the Stoics did, was no small service to humanity.

But there are other and more practical benefits directly traceable to this view of life. By laying stress on what was common to all mankind, viz., his rationality, instead of on what was particular, viz., his circumstances and individual capacities, this theory laid the foundations for a new view of the relations of men to one another. Hence it was in the Stoic schools that the idea of the brotherhood of man, as opposed to the partnership of citizens, first took root, and was made the basis of the denial of the distinction between slave and free.* It might be said that it was to Christianity and not to Stoicism that the general acceptance of this idea was due. This is doubtless true:† but that the early Christians conceived it in a mystic and emotional, rather than a reflective and practical form, is seen in the fact that slavery as a human institution rouses no protest in the first writers.

But his rational nature is not only that which unites man to man: it is also that which gives to each his separate dignity as a man. In emphasising it, Stoicism laid the foundations of the conception of human personality, and thus provided, for the first time, a secure basis for a consistent theory of legal rights. Hence it was that a doc-

---

* The first protest against the institution of slavery seems to have come from the Cynics. See Zeller's *Socrates and the Socratic Schools*, p. 323.   † See pp. 231, 232.

trine, which as a principle of morals has too often been stark and barren, blossomed in the field of politics under the fostering care of Stoic thinkers into the great system of rights and obligations known as Roman Law.

§ 55. Duty for Duty's Sake as a Practical Principle

In actual practice the theory that lays the emphasis upon duty, as opposed to inclination, contains an important element of truth, which naturalistic theories of the end of action have always tended to overlook. For it is undoubtedly true that at a certain stage in moral development, both in the individual and in the race, the negative or ascetic element is the prominent one. All moral progress consists in subordination of lower to higher impulses, and at a certain stage it may be more important to conquer the lower than to give effect to the higher. How far it is possible to effect this conquest without appeal to higher and more positive principles of action; how far, for instance, sensual impulses can be made to yield before the abstract announcements of reason that they are "wrong," without assignment of further reason or without appeal to the higher interests and affections, is a question for the educator. What is certain is, that morality begins in self-restraint and self-denial, and that it is impossible to conceive of circumstances in which this negative element will be totally absent from it. Whatever we are to say of the desire to enjoy pleasure, it is certain that readiness to suffer pain is an element in all virtue, and that there is more danger for the individual in indulging the former than in over-cultivating the latter.*

* At a time when ethical theories are anti-ascetic rather than hedonistic, it is delightful, in a scientific treatise, to come across a passage like the following on the practical value of ἄσκησις: " As

The defect of the ascetic theory is not that it lays emphasis on the negative aspect of morality, but that it treats that aspect as the final one. Self-realisation cannot consist in mere resistance to the suggestions of desire. If it did, the satisfaction of one element in human nature would mean the destruction of another; the realisation of reason would mean the annihilation of feeling and desire. Seeing, moreover, that virtue consists in free determination by reason, and reason is not otherwise definable on this theory save as the antithesis of desire, the virtuous man, so far from being independent of desire, is dependent on its continued resistance for the opportunity of realising himself in conflict with it. Virtue, in fact, lives in the life of its antagonist. Final and complete victory over it would involve its own destruction along with the destruction of desire.* This, which might be

a final practical maxim, relative to these habits of the will, we may, then, offer something like this: *Keep the faculty of effort alive in you by a little gratuitous exercise every day.* That is, be systematically ascetic or heroic in little unnecessary points; do every day or two something for no other reason than that you would rather not do it: so that, when the hour of dire need draws nigh, it may find you not unnerved and untrained to stand the test. Asceticism of this sort is like the insurance which a man pays on his house and goods. The tax does him no good at the time, and possibly may never bring him a return. But, if the fire does come, his having paid it will be his salvation from ruin. So with the man who has daily inured himself to habits of concentrated attention, energetic volition, and self-denial in unnecessary things. He will stand like a tower when everything rocks round him, and when his softer fellow-mortals are winnowed like chaff in the blast."—Prof. William James's *Principles of Psychology*, Vol. I., p. 126. On the subject of the paragraph generally, *cp.* Dewey, *op. cit.*, pp. 94, 155, 156.

* This one-sidedness might be further illustrated from the dependence of the ascetic for the *feeling* or *sense* of self-realisation upon

called the "paradox of asceticism," is the explanation
of the failure which has attended all attempts to organise
a practical scheme of life upon the basis of this theory.
In the absence of an inspiring positive ideal of human
life, those who have been in earnest about the matter
have alternately been occupied with the vain attempt
to cancel in themselves all healthy human interests, or
(failing, as they were bound to do, to realise this ideal)
with counselling * that retirement from the conflict which
death alone can offer. The less earnest spirits to whom
this ideal has been offered have tended, on the other
hand, to fall back, with true cynical indifference, upon
the lowest forms of sensual life.†

§ 56. Criticism of Theory

The practical difficulty suggested by the Hedonistic
theory was, as we saw, that it fails to afford any secure
foundation for the distinction between right and wrong.
The vocabulary of "right" (duty, obligation, responsibility, ought) seems to have no place in psychological
Hedonism. The objection to the opposite theory may,

the consciousness of what he is *not* rather than of what he is, *i.e.*,
upon the contrast between himself and others. Hence, that which
in ordinary cases is the approval of conscience becomes in him an
odious species of spiritual pride. This is illustrated in the well-
known stories of Diogenes, as when he mocked Plato for pride of
dress and bearing, and got the answer, " I see thy pride, Diogenes,
through the holes in thy cloak." *Cp.* Shakespeare's *Timon of
Athens :*—
   Tɪᴍᴏɴ. "Thou art proud, Apemantus."
   Aᴘ.   "Of nothing so much as that I am not like Timon."
   * As did the Roman Stoics.
   † As was illustrated by the history of the Cynics (see Zeller's
Socrates and the Socratic Schools) and the mediæval monasteries.

as we have just seen, be said to be the opposite one.
It fails to provide for the ordinary daily life of humanity.
If no act is morally right which is done because we *desire*
to do it, then, not only because I am virtuous am I to
have no more cakes and ale, but a stain is cast on all
conduct which in the common intercourse of life springs
spontaneously from the ordinary affections of love and
pity, hope and fear. The source of those two opposite
errors is the place which is assigned to reason by each
respectively. In the one case reason gives no end at
all, but is confined to the function of prescribing the
means for realising the end set by the sentient nature.
In the other case it provides indeed an end, but, in
denying human desire a place in the good life, it
denies the only means by which the ideal end can
ever pass into actuality. But while the view before
us presents these points of contrast with the preceding
one in regard to the function it assigns to thought or
reason, it is in fundamental agreement with it in holding
that reason stands outside the object of desire, and is
only externally related to it. On the one theory as on
the other, the object is conceived of as given by the
appetitive or purely irrational part of our nature : the
only object of desire is pleasure, and in desiring pleasure
man is determined by his sentient or appetitive nature
alone.

In criticism of this view of the relation of reason to
desire it must be pointed out :—(1) that there can be
no object of desire, in the proper sense of the word,
which is not constituted such by reason itself. This
was involved in our analysis of desire. To refuse to recognise it is to confuse the distinction between appetite
and desire. The lower animals have appetites and are

determined by them, but we have no reason to attribute to them the power of conceiving objects of desire. On the other hand, man also is said to have appetites, but these are only the raw material of desire, as sensation may be said to be the raw material of perception. So soon as we became conscious of them as elements which compete for the determination of our conduct, they have ceased to be mere appetites in becoming desires, just as the sensation of which we are conscious as an element in knowledge is no longer a mere sensation, but an object of perception.

(2) As there can be no desire without the conscious activity of thought or reason, so there can be no activity in a thinking or rational self (as we understand such activity) without desire. The idea that there can could only have arisen in the confusion just criticised between appetite and desire. It is perfectly true that reason may oppose the blind impulses of animal appetite, and that such opposition must always be the first step in the moral life. But this does not mean that the rational life is therefore the life which is undetermined by desire, but that it is the life which is habitually regulated with a view to the satisfaction of the higher or more universal as opposed to the lower or more particular desires. Even in its highest and apparently purest manifestations, as, for instance, in the search for truth, reason is determined by interest, *i.e.*, by feeling and desire. The rational life, in such a case, consists not in acting independently of desire,—this is impossible,—but in subordinating the lower or more particular desires (*e.g.*, the desire to amass wealth for oneself and family) to the higher and more universal (*e.g.*, the discovery of truth and the benefit of the species).

(3) If it be asked according to what law or principle this relative subordination of desires is to be effected, if not according to the principle, laid down by the theory criticised, of determination by reason alone, we are brought back to the question of our present investigation,—the question of the standard of the relative merit or value of conduct. Without yet attempting to summarise our results upon the whole question, I may here point out that, even from the side of the lower life of the so-called animal appetites, we are not left without a witness. For these appetites, even in the lower animals, are not the blind chaos of lawless elements which the theory we are considering supposes them to be. They are already organised according to a law or reason of their own,—the law, namely, of the subordination of those which are less important for the ends of the individual or the species (if you like, the lower) to those which are more important (if you like, the higher). It is not, of course, meant that the life of the lower animals or of man in his "natural" state is explicitly rational, but that the so-called "animal impulses" themselves do not present us with a chaos of disorderly elements, but already constitute a *system*, in which a relative subordination to an implicit end is distinctly traceable. How this end is to be defined is as much a question for biology as for ethics. It may at this point be described, in biological language, as adaptation to environment, or the establishment of equilibrium between function and the field in which it is called upon to act.* To pursue this end in one form or another is the law of all sentient

---

* The question whether this equilibrium is that of the particular individual, or of the tribe or species (*i.e.*, whether it is individual or social), will come up in another form at a later stage in this analysis.

life. The difference between man and the lower orders
of creation is not that law, which is only implicit reason,
first manifests itself in him, but that he first becomes
aware of it as such; or, as it is sometimes expressed,
reason first becomes aware of itself in him. It is, of
course, true that in becoming conscious of himself as
subject to this law, or as called upon to realise this end,
man has lost his primitive innocence,—he has eaten of
the tree of knowledge, and *knows* good and evil. But
this does not mean that he has to evolve the law of
duty and of right from his own inner consciousness. It
only means that he is henceforth called upon to pursue
consciously the end which sub-human nature pursues
unconsciously, to make explicit in his own life the
reason already implicitly contained in it.

(4) Hence the end or standard of good action cannot be
the suppression of the desires, but co-ordination of them
as each in its place capable of contributing to realise the
end of the whole, yet strictly subordinate to it. Such is
the constitution of human life, that the satisfaction of the
higher desires is only possible by means of the relative
satisfaction of the lower. Thus the gratification of the
desire for knowledge, to revert to our previous example,
is only possible in any society, and, in a sense, by any
individual, on condition that the more primary instinct
to acquire property and secure the means of subsistence
has been satisfied. Hence it is that even the lower
desires bring with them their own justification. The
function of reason is not to eliminate, but to transform
them.*

* On the subject of this paragraph, see Bradley, *op. cit.*, Essay IV.;
Caird, *op. cit.*, Vol. II., Book II., ch. ii., esp. pp. 202-209, 226-8;
Dewey, *op. cit.*, pp. 84-96, also pp. 23, 24.

CHAPTER III

EVOLUTIONARY HEDONISM

§ 57. Utilitarianism and Evolution

THE utilitarian theory has recently been taken up by some of the leading exponents of biological evolution, chiefly Mr. Herbert Spencer, and has from them received a new form, which we must next consider. It is important to observe the precise point of divergence between the newer and the older form of the pleasure theory. The objections urged against the latter by the former do not concern the nature of the end, or that which, in the last resort, is the standard of value in moral judgments. This is still the same. "No school," says Mr. Spencer, "can avoid taking for the ultimate moral aim a desirable state of feeling, called by whatever name, gratification, enjoyment, happiness. Pleasure, somewhere, at some time, to some being or beings, is an inexpugnable element in the conception." * But while this is so, the presuppositions on which the older form of utilitarianism rested, and the method which it employed, are thought to be open to serious objection.

Thus, it is pointed out that the older form is founded

* *Data of Ethics*, § 15. *Cp.* Appendix, p. 307 (5th ed.).

on an erroneous conception of man's nature. The writers who founded and developed utilitarianism, in its earlier forms, started from a conception of the relation of the individual to his social environment which, in view of the results now established, is quite untenable. (1) It regards society as an aggregate of individuals, mechanically cohering, like atoms or molecules in inorganic matter. The weakness of this point of view became obvious when the question was asked how the atoms or molecules of which society, on this theory, consists, came together at all. It was to meet this question that recourse was had by earlier writers to the myth of the "Social Contract," according to which individuals, who had previously lived in isolation, at length came together; and in order to secure the greater good of self-preservation, contracted themselves out of their natural rights to freedom and equality. (2) Corresponding to this conception of society as an aggregate of homogeneous units, we have the conception of fixed and equal "lots" of happiness. "We must conceive of happiness" (according to this theory) "as a kind of emotional currency, capable of being calculated and distributed in 'lots,' which have a certain definite value independently of any special taste of the individual. . . . Pains and pleasures can be handed about like pieces of money, and we have simply to calculate how to gain a maximum of pleasure and a minimum of pain."* (3) It looks at society as static. The atoms are relatively constant. It is true that they vary according to the circumstances of birth and education. But these variations are, as it were, accidental and individual. On the aggregate, they remain the same.

---

* Leslie Stephen, *Science of Ethics*, p. 360.

(4) The happiness or pleasure, to cause and distribute which so as to secure the greatest amount to the greatest number is the moral end, is similarly conceived of as relative only to the capacities of individuals statically considered. Its main features are fixed by the constitution of human nature as at present empirically known to us.

§ 58. The Organic View of Human Society corrects these Errors

For this "atomic theory" of human nature and happiness, modern science has substituted the organic. Go back, it teaches, as far as you will, in the history of the race or of the individual, you never come to anything that in any degree corresponds to the "individual" of the older theories. We never know man but as a member of some kind of society. He not only exists in a society, but is what he is in virtue of his relation to it. The connection between the individual and society is not merely external and mechanical, but internal and organic. All that makes him what he is, all his powers of mind and body, are inherited, *i.e.*, come to him from a previous state of society. The instincts and desires which are the springs of his actions presuppose some sort of organised society of family and tribe as the field of their satisfaction. The education which he receives is only possible by means of such social institutions as language, the family, the school, the workshop. The prizes he wins in battle, the property he acquires in trade, can only be secured to him in virtue of some form of social law and social justice, however rudimentary. In a word, his life takes its form at every point from the relation in which he stands to his social environment.

All this is expressed in the scientific doctrine which has superseded the myth of the social contract as the ground of explanation of the phenomena of morals and politics.* "A full perception of the truth," says Mr. Leslie Stephen, "that society is not a mere aggregate, but an organic growth,—that it forms a whole the laws of whose growth can be studied apart from those of the individual atom,—supplies the most characteristic postulate of modern speculation." "Society, in fact, is a structure which by its nature implies a certain fixity in the distribution and relations of classes. Each man is found with a certain part of the joint framework, which is made of flesh and blood instead of bricks or timber, but which is not the less truly a persistent structure."†

But society is not only an organism in the sense that the form of the individual life is determined by his relation to the whole, as the various members are by their relation to the body,‡ but in the sense that, like other organisms, it grows and develops by reaction upon its environment. This growth is a simultaneous process of

* I speak in the text as though scientific writers had an equal hold of the notion that society is an organism, and expounded it with equal insight. As a matter of fact, a history of the doctrine would show that writers greatly differ in these respects. Mr. Spencer, who might be said to have been the founder of it, holds it with a feeble grasp (see D. G. Ritchie's criticisms, *Principles of State Interference*, I. and II.), and expounds it (*Essays*, Vol. I.) in an external way, as though it were an interesting "analogy" or metaphor. On the other hand, Mr. Stephen, as quoted in the text, has made a great advance on all previous statements of this truth in this country.

† Leslie Stephen's *Science of Ethics*, pp. 31, 29.

‡ "We might as well regard the members of our own body as animals," says Mr. James Ward, " as suppose man is man apart from humanity."

differentiation and integration, the structure acquiring greater complexity, and the individuals becoming more dependent upon one another. The end of the process is expressed in various ways as "increase," "development," "greatest totality," of life. "Evolution," says Mr. Spencer, "reaches its limit when individual life is the greatest, both in length and *breadth*."

Finally, the law of social evolution is the law of evolution in other fields: that society survives which, owing to the constitution of its parts and members, and their faithfulness in the discharge of their individual functions, is best adapted to its environment. It is the pressure of the environment (*e.g.*, of one tribe upon another in the struggle for existence) which explains the survival of those communities in which conduct is best adapted to the end of social preservation, *i.e.*, furthers the health and strength of the tribe or nation. Hence, "social evolution means the evolution of a strong social tissue;* the best type is the type implied by the strongest tissue."

When these results are applied to the theory of pleasure, and of moral judgment founded upon it, they are seen to imply important consequences. Pleasure is seen to depend, not upon the constitution of the individual considered as an isolated atom, but upon the "organic balance" of the individual's own instincts, as this is determined by his relations to society. "Pleasure is not a separate thing, independently of his special organisation. . . . Each instinct, for example, must have its turn, and their respective provinces must be determined by

---

* Mr. Stephen prefers "social tissue" to "social organism," because a nation has not the unity of the *higher organisms*. It is limited by external circumstances, not, like them, by internal constitution. See *op. cit.*, ch. iii., § 31.

the general organic balance. We may undoubtedly point
out that certain modes of conduct produce pain, and
others pleasure; and this is a *primâ facie* reason, at least,
for avoiding one and accepting the other. But, again,
some pains imply a remedial process, while others imply
disease; and the conduct which increases them may
therefore either be wise or foolish in the highest
degree." *

Similarly, the fact of growth and evolution in the social
organism involves a revision of our conception of happiness. Development implies the acquisition of new
instincts and desires. Hence the happiness (resulting
from the satisfactions of desires) which satisfies at one
stage ceases to satisfy at another. "Happiness itself
changes as the society develops, and we cannot compare
the two societies at different stages, as if they were
more or less efficient machines for obtaining an identical
product."

§ 59. On the Utilitarian Theory Moral Laws are Empirical Generalisations

Hence the further criticism of the method recognised
by utilitarianism that it is empirical. Morality is a generalisation founded on collated instances from ordinary
experience as to the best means of producing the greatest
sum-total of pleasure. To the evolutionist, on the other
hand, morality is the condition of health in the organism.
It is "the definition of some of the most important qualities of the social organism." "The moral law defines a
property of the social tissue" †—the property that makes
for its health. The imperatives, "Thou shalt not steal,"

* *Science of Ethics*, p. 365.
† *Science of Ethics*, pp. 148, 168.

"Thou shalt not commit adultery," are not to be justified on the ground that the greatest happiness to ourselves and others may be shown by appeal to experience to result from obeying them (this may or may not be so demonstrable), but because they are essential to the vitality and efficiency of the organism. "This represents the real difference between the utilitarian and the evolutionist criterion. The one lays down as a criterion the happiness, the other, the health, of the society."

The two are not, however, really opposed. On the contrary, the health of society is only valuable as the condition of its happiness. The difference between evolutionary ethics and Hedonism is not in the ultimate end they severally recommend, but in the proximate one. It does not concern the object to be reached by man, but the method of reaching it. The end is happiness, but that is best attained by keeping it in the background, and fixing attention upon the conditions. "While I admit," says Mr. Spencer,* "that happiness is the ultimate end to be contemplated, I do not admit that it should be the proximate end. . . . I conceive it to be the business of moral science to deduce from the laws of life and the conditions of existence what kinds of action necessarily tend to produce happiness, and what kinds to produce unhappiness. Having done this, its deductions are to be recognised as laws of conduct, and are to be conformed to irrespective of a direct estimation of happiness or misery." Finally, as illustrations of the blunders into which the application of the empirical or direct method may lead us, Mr. Spencer has drawn up a formidable list of mistaken efforts at legislation for the

* *Data of Ethics*, § 21.

greatest happiness of the greatest number within the past few decades.*

So far we have the criticism of the older utilitarians by their evolutionist brethren of to-day. Let us now examine the value of the criticism, and the position which the critics have left to themselves.

§ 60. Importance of Theory of Evolution in the Field of Ethics

The value of the results which issue from the application of the theory of evolution in the field of ethics can hardly be overrated. To mention a few of the gains that we owe more or less directly to it we may note that:—

(1) *It makes individualistic presuppositions untenable.* It shows the theories already criticised to be as untenable from a biological as we have seen that they are from an ethical point of view. These theories in all their forms are individualistic, *i.e.*, the self whose satisfaction is the ethical end is conceived of as isolated, or at any rate as not essentially related to society. Thus the Cyrenaics, while urging the pleasures of social intercourse, took care to add that one was to practise the art of living together "like a stranger." The Epicureans extolled in this respect friendship, the most subjective and accidental of social bonds.† The same defect hardly needs illustration from modern Hedonism. In the older forms, as in Hobbes,‡ the self is one whose satisfaction may not only be attained independently of society, but is actually crossed in its completeness by

---

* See *The Man* versus *The State*, pp. 7 foll. (8th ed.).
† See Erdmann's *History of Philosophy*, Vol. I., pp. 90, 185.
‡ Who starts from the axiom *homo homini lupus*.

the existence of society.   In later Hedonism we have
already seen the shifts to which its supporters are reduced, to stretch their egoistic basis so as to cover the
facts of ordinary morality and social life.

The same feature appears in all the forms of the
opposite theory with which we made a passing acquaintance in discussing "duty for duty's sake."   The Cynic
and the Stoic aimed at being independent of the social,
as of other instincts and desires, the former deliberately
cultivating a form of unsociableness which has passed
into a byword, the latter living in times when social
and political life no longer offered scope for the higher
aspirations of the soul, and men were forced to seek in
the inner life for the satisfaction that the world denied
them.   Similarly the "world" with which the Christian
ascetic waged war included the relationships of family,
society, and state; and even to Kant, society is the
field of the reign of interests hostile to true self-
determination.*

On each and all of these theories, society is conceived
of as consisting of a mechanical union of mutually
repellent particles, each of which pursues an end to
which the others stand at best as means.   On the other
hand, the individuals are conceived of as independent
of society, and only submitting to its restraints on the

---

* Of course it is impossible to secure the independence aimed at
by those who adopted this attitude.   Diogenes, however poorly he
thought of society, was glad, at any rate, to have the contrast, only
possible by means of it, between himself and others.   Simeon Stylites
does not appear to have been indifferent to the admiration of by-
standers.   In the nobler forms of the theory, notably in Kant's
philosophy, its individualism is always on the verge of breaking
down (see Caird, *loc. cit.*).

fuller life they might otherwise enjoy, in virtue either of necessity or of the greater general security to the vital interests of persons and property that it brings.

Amid much confusion (to be shortly referred to), evolutionist writers have helped to bring home the truth that the "self," whose satisfaction upon these theories is in one form or another the end, is an abstraction. No attempt to define it in terms of its individual nature as only accidentally related to society can henceforth succeed.

(2) *It shows how moral ideas have had a history.* Its contribution to the proper understanding of the history of moral judgments and of forms of virtue has been not less valuable. Just as the application of scientific ideas in the field of sociology makes the older forms, both of naturalistic and rationalist theories of the end, untenable, so the application of the historic method to the theory of conscience, and the forms which morality takes in different countries and times, puts Intuitionalism * out of court. In view of the facts brought forward, it can no longer be maintained that the judgments of conscience are innate and underived principles, related to the circumstances only as the field in which effect

---

* Mr. Spencer professes to have reconciled scientific with intuitionalist ethics. "The evolution hypothesis enables us to reconcile opposed moral theories. . . . For . . . the doctrine of innate powers of moral perception becomes congruous with the utilitarian doctrine, when it is seen that preferences and aversions are rendered organic by inheritance of the effects of pleasurable and painful experiences in progenitors."—*Data of Ethics*, p. 124; see whole passage, with which *cp. Social Statics*, Introduction (and see Dewey, *op. cit.*, p. 69). This kind of reconciliation reminds one of the cynic's witty interpretation of the manner in which the lion and the lamb shall lie down together. according to prophecy.

is to be given to them. They are shown to be vitally related to the stage of development at which the society whose morality they represent has arrived, and to have had a history in time like all other forms of conscious life. This "relativity" of the standard will be the subject of a future chapter, and need not further detain us here.

(3) *It throws new light on the place of pleasure in ethics.* A flood of fresh light has been shed on the place of pleasure in biological evolution, and on the physiological causes which have led to its being, as we have already defined it to be, the "feeling of self-realisedness." It is shown that, in as much as creatures tend to persist in pleasurable activities, those will tend to survive in the struggle for existence in which pleasurable activities are in harmony with the environment, and therefore tend to further life; those, on the other hand, will tend to perish in which pleasurable activities are hostile to the organism by being unsuited to its environment. In this way pleasure, on the whole, will come to be the accompaniment of activities which tend to the survival, pains of activities which tend to the destruction of the organism. In man that which corresponds to the former species of activities is, of course, moral conduct; that which corresponds to the latter, immoral conduct. Whence it follows that moral conduct tends to be accompanied by pleasure, immoral conduct by pain.* The gain to ethics generally from this account of pleasure is to be measured by the strength of the tendency, which has asserted itself in all ages, to regard pleasure as a delusion of sense, and by its nature hostile to the moral life. Such a view is no longer consistent with the elementary facts of biology.

* See *Data of Ethics*, § 33.

§ 61. Difficulties in Evolutionary Ethics

(1) *The Hedonistic hypothesis which it favours finds no support in biology.* The difficulties and questions which this theory raises centre round the uncritical alliance which it has formed with the pleasure theory (see p. 125). The Hedonistic assumption is so confidently embraced by Mr. Spencer, that it might be supposed that biology had brought new facts to its support. We may, therefore, first ask whether biology has brought to light any new facts which might support the main contention of psychological Hedonism that pleasure is the only thing desired. Now so far is this from being the case, that the conclusions of biology go on all fours with the results of our previous criticism of this theory. They show that impulse and desire precede the feeling of pleasure, and not *vice versâ*. Pleasure indeed follows upon successful effort: it is the sign of it; but the impulse or desire to exercise the function precedes and conditions the pleasure, not *vice versâ*. In human life the object gives us pleasure, in the first instance, because we desire it; we do not desire it because it gives us pleasure.* We may, of course, make the pleasure our object. We may use the

---

* This is the explanation of the so-called " paradox of Hedonism," viz., that the only way to secure pleasure is not to aim at it (see Mill's *Autobiography*, p. 142). It is really its refutation. For an early statement of this truth, see Butler's *Sermons*, XI.: "That all particular appetites and passions are towards *external things themselves*, distinct from the *pleasure arising from them*, is manifest from hence; that there could not be this pleasure were it not for that prior suitableness between the object and the passion: there could be no enjoyment or delight from one thing more than another, from eating food more than from swallowing a stone, if there were not an affection or appetite to one thing more than another."

organs (*e.g.*, of taste and digestion) in order to enjoy
the pleasure of the exercise of their functions. But
this is unnatural, and, in the strict sense of the word,
"preposterous." Nature herself protests against it by
impairing and, if we persist, destroying the organs:
perhaps ourselves along with them.

Nor can it be replied that, though desire must precede
the *feeling of pleasure*, yet desire itself is the result of felt
uneasiness, and is therefore, even its most primitive form,
an effort to escape from pain. For the natural instinct
or longing is itself again the condition of the felt pain,
not *vice versâ*. It is, of course, true, as we have already
seen,* that the "tension" between the pain of the present
state, and the pleasure of the anticipated realisation of
the object desired, is an element in the phenomenon
of desire, and that this tension may itself be said to
be predominantly painful; but what is maintained is,
that this pain, in so far as it is an element in desire,
is conditional on the natural instinct or impulse towards
the object, and not *vice versâ*. We may, of course,
make the escape from pain or uneasiness the motive
of an act, just as we may make pleasure our motive;
but this is not a .normal motive of action, and in the
ordinary round of daily activities, and especially in the
higher forms of activity, as in scientific investigation or
artistic production, it can hardly be said to have a place
at all.

(2) *On the Hedonistic assumption, "Increase of Life"
cannot be proved to be desirable.* But setting this psychological question aside, and admitting that there may
be other objects of desire besides personal pleasure,

---

* See p. 47.

it is still contended by the supporter of the view under discussion that the ultimate end which all seek is the greatest pleasure. What gives value to that "increase of life" which, as the end of evolution, is to be the portion of the "completely adapted man in the completely evolved society," is the increase of pleasure which it brings with it.

Now, in reference to this contention, it might be asked whether, as a matter of fact, this "increase of life" does bring increase of happiness. Are the more highly developed nations and individuals "happier" than the less developed. It might indeed be argued that the greater the variety of powers and capacities developed in mankind, the greater the capacities of enjoyment. But that is just the point that is contested; and, as is well known, an influential philosophy has been built upon the opposite theory, that "he that increaseth knowledge increaseth sorrow." Without subscribing to Pessimism,* we may fairly doubt whether more highly developed powers of mind and conscience necessarily bring with them increase of happiness. It is quite certain that they are apt to throw the individual or the nation possessing them into situations where the sacrifice of happiness seems to be required; so that, as Mr. Stephen admits, to exhort a man to virtue may be "to exhort him to acquire a faculty which will, in many cases, make him less fit than the less moral man for getting the greatest amount of happiness from a given combination of circumstances." And generally it may be questioned whether, besides the two dimensions of life which Mr. Spencer mentions as belonging to it at its highest development, "length and

---

* As has been wittily said, " If Pessimism be true, it differs from other truths by its uselessness."

breadth," * there is not a third, viz., depth, which, whatever we are to say of the others, may be a *minus* quantity as regards pleasure, and anything that could go by
the name of happiness.†

Nor can it be said in reply that the pain which such
highly developed types involve is the result of social
maladjustment, which *ex hypothesi* is excluded in a
society where a perfect equilibrium between function
and environment has been established.   For, again, this
hypothesis is open to grave doubt.   Can it be
shown that progress *is* towards such a state of stable
equilibrium?   Is such a "completely adapted man" as
Mr. Spencer supposes ‡ a possible conception?   That
progress means the establishment of equilibrium between
ever higher and more differentiated functions in society
and the individual is undoubted: but it is equally undoubted that in each case the equilibrium is established
only to be broken into again by new forces which have
to be equilibrated, new differences that have to be
reconciled.   Of an absolute and final equilibrium of the
kind demanded, from which pain and conflict will be

---

* *Data of Ethics*, p. 25.

† "Odd," says the doctor in Margaret Deland's clever novel
Sydney, "that it is the sight of trouble which makes me want to
live more earnestly; for the deeper you live, the more trouble you
have.   But I suppose trouble is a man's birthright, and instinct
makes him seek it."   *Cp.* passage quoted from *Romola*, in Green's
Proleg. to Ethics, p. 404 *n.*

‡ See the whole chapter on "Absolute and Relative Ethics" in
Data of Ethics, with which may be compared the earlier and more
uncompromising statement of the same doctrine, *Social Statics*,
Part I., ch. i.   For a criticism of it see Sidgwick's *Methods of
Ethics*, Book I., ch. ii., § 2, and art. in *Mind*, XVIII., pp. 222-6.
See also p. 141 *n.* below.

excluded, evolution knows nothing. The only analogue
to it in nature is death. Where there is life there is
progress. In death alone (individual or national) there
is final equilibrium. Here alone there is no change and
development in the organism, requiring readjustment to
an environment which is different because the organism
is different. In regard to social progress, we have no
warrant for believing that individual aspiration after a
higher form of life than the environment admits of will
not keep pace with the progress already attained, and that
struggle and sacrifice, with the pain that they involve,
will not be the permanent portion of the more highly
developed, *i.e.*, the more moral, individuals.*

But even though we admit the possibility of a society
so completely adapted to its environment, and consisting
of will so completely harmonised with one another, that
every element of pain, even that expressed by the word
obligation,† will disappear, it might still be questioned
whether such a society is one which man, as man, can
take as his ideal. If it be true that man by his nature
is progressive, that the strain and accompanying un-
pleasantness of the endeavour to realise himself in ever
higher forms is a necessary element in his life and not
merely a transitory accident; if it be true that it is of
the essence of man to be

> " hurled
> From change to change unceasingly,
> His soul's wings never furled,"—

then the scientific Utopia of Mr. Spencer may prove, as

* The above argument must not be interpreted as intended to
prove that development is not desirable, but merely that, *on the Hedonistic hypothesis*, it is not possible to prove its desirableness.

† See *Data of Ethics*, § 46 fin.

a moral ideal, to be as uninviting and inoperative as the
economic paradise of M. Godin* or Mr. Bellamy, or the
"Nowhere" from which Mr. Morris brings us news.†

(3) *Defect of Method having its source in failure to
distinguish Science of Causes and Science of Ends.* A
third and more serious question is suggested by the
claim that is put forward by evolutionary ethics to be
"rational," as opposed to the older form of utilitarianism, which is "empirical." ‡ For when we inquire what
the critics have to say in turn of the evolutionists'
theory, we find that this is precisely the objection which
they urge against it: it is empirical or experimental, as
opposed to the view which they themselves support.§

In order to understand the force of this objection it
is necessary to inquire more precisely than we have
hitherto done into what is meant by the claim put
forward by the evolutionist writers to have advanced
beyond empiricism, and to have set morality on a rational
basis. Mr. Spencer is at pains to explain his meaning.
As opposed to early or empirical science, he points out

---

* See Gronlund's criticism, *Our Destiny*, ch. i., § 8.

† Besides the other advance (mentioned p. 128 *n.*) which marks
Mr. Stephen's presentation of evolutionary ethics, it possesses the
further advantage over Mr. Spencer's in relegating absolute or Utopian
ethics to the lumber-room of ethical speculation. "The attempt
to establish an absolute coincidence between virtue and happiness
is in ethics what the attempting to square the circle or to discover
perpetual motion is in geometry or mechanics" (*Science of Ethics,*
p. 430). Mr. Alexander (*Moral Order and Progress*, pp. 266 foll.)
criticises it even more severely as founded on a misconception of
the meaning of "adaptation to environment."

‡ *Data of Ethics*, 1st Ed., p. 312, and elsewhere.

§ See Sorley's *Ethics of Naturalism*, ch. ix.; Courtney's *Constructive Ethics*, p. 273, and elsewhere.

that all developed science may be characterised as *a priori* or rational, "if the drawing of deductions from premisses positively ascertained by induction is to be so called." He illustrates the distinction from the case of astronomy: "During its early stages, planetary astronomy consisted of nothing more than accumulated observations respecting the positions and motions of the sun and planets, from which accumulated observations it came by-and-by to be empirically predicted, with an approach to truth, that certain of the heavenly bodies would have certain positions at certain times. But the modern science of planetary astronomy consists of deductions from the law of gravitation,—deductions showing why the celestial bodies *necessarily* occupy certain places at certain times. Now the kind of relation which thus exists between ancient and modern astronomy is analogous to the kind of relation which I conceive exists between the expediency morality, and moral science properly so called." The distinction here referred to is familiar to the student of logic.* A simpler instance of it is the difference between the discovery by direct experiment, *e.g.*, upon a billiard ball, that two forces of a given magnitude acting upon it at a given angle to one another produce movement bearing a certain uniform relation to their respective direction and amount, and the inference, drawn from the known law of the effect of each of the forces taken singly, as to what will be the law of their joint effect. The former is an empirical generalisation, the latter is a deduction.

Now it is to be observed that this distinction lies within the field of what are commonly called the natural

* See especially Mill's *Logic*, Book III., ch. ix.

sciences, *i.e.*, the sciences which deal with the laws of causal connection between natural phenomena. It refers to different modes of arriving at these laws. By the term empirical is meant the method of simple observation, without analysis of the phenomenon under investigation into its constituent elements; by the term deductive, ratiocinative, or *a priori*, the method which proceeds from the real or supposed laws of the action of each constituent taken separately to deduce the law of their action when combined.

But there is another sense of the word "empirical" in which it is applied to those sciences which deal with efficient causes, *i.e.*, with results effected by a *vis a tergo*, as opposed to those which deal with ends or final causes —with the effects of the thought or idea of a *terminus ad quem*. In this sense all the sciences, which deal with phenomena as such, are empirical; those, on the other hand, which deal with phenomena *as intended*, *i.e.*, as consciously conceived in reference to an end, are teleological or rational. Instances of the former are physics and biology in all their branches; instances of the latter, ethics, politics, and the theories of art, knowledge, and religion. This all-important distinction has not been sufficiently recognised by evolutionist writers. Entangling themselves at the outset with the assumption that the actions of men are determined, like those of animals, by *pleasures and pains as by efficient causes*, instead of by the *idea of an end*, *i.e.*, by a final cause, they have confused the issue, and are still open to the charge of being empirical, though in a different and more serious sense. "'The doctrine of evolution itself,'" it has been well said, "when added to empirical morality, only widens our view of the old landscape—does not enable us to pass from 'is' to 'ought,' or from efficient to final cause, any more than the telescope can point beyond the sphere of spatial quantity."*

We have already seen how the moral laws which are the "data of ethics" can only spring from such a conception of an end. We have further seen how such an end must be a personal good, *i.e.*, the realisation or satisfaction of the self. Lastly, we have seen how this satisfaction cannot be sought in any mere state of feeling. The last result is practically accepted by the evolutionist, when he proposes to substitute for greatest pleasure the end of "social health" or "increase of life." But in rejecting this element of error in the older utilitarianism, he has also dropped the element of truth which it represented, viz., that the end must be a form of *personal* good.† It is perfectly open to him to point out, as none have done so admirably, that the "person" cannot be conceived of as an isolated atom, and that the end cannot be the isolated gratification of any one or of any number of such atoms; but this only means that the "good" of the individual must be also a common good. It cannot mean that the good is not a personal one. If it does, the theory simply means that it is impossible to deduce any moral law from the conception of end, *i.e.*, to have any science of ethics in the proper sense. Yet this is precisely the difficulty in which evolutionary ethics, in the writings of its leading exponents, has landed us. Our objection to their conclusions is not that they apply evolution to conscience

---

* Sorley, *op. cit.*, p. 273. *Cp.* Sidgwick's art. on "Mr. Spencer's Ethical System," *Mind*, XVIII.

† For criticisms founded on this defect see Royce, *Religious Aspect of Philosophy*, pp. 74-85; Dewey, *op. cit.*, pp. 71-8.

and the forms of morality, still less that they widen our view of the nature of self and give us a new insight into the nature of pleasure, but that they cling to the empirical point of view, and so fail to get the full meaning out of their own results. The "health," "vitality," "adaptation," or what not, "of the social organism," are valuable *formulæ* in helping us to define the contents of "the good." As anything more, they are abstractions without relation to the moral end.

What is required to complete the evolutionist theory is (1) once and for all to renounce Hedonism and all its works; (2) to add to its empirical demonstration that the individual is essentially social a teleological demonstration that his good is essentially a common good. In a previous chapter we showed the way in respect to the former, the next chapter will deal with the latter desideratum.

Note.

In illustration of the defect of evolutionary ethics which is pointed out in the text, the important admissions made by Mr. Stephen in his section on Self-Sacrifice, *op. cit.*, p. 426 onward, may be quoted: " When we say to a man, 'This is right,' we cannot also say invariably and unhesitatingly, 'This will be for your happiness.' The cold-hearted and grovelling nature has an argument which, from its own point of view, is not only victorious in practice, but logically unanswerable. Not only is it impossible to persuade people to do right always,—a matter of fact as to which there is not likely to be much dispute,—but there is no argument in existence which, if exhibited to them, would always appear to be conclusive. A thoroughly selfish man prefers to spend money on gratifying his own senses which might save some family from misery and starvation. He prefers to do so, let us say, even at the cost of breaking some recognised obligation—of telling a lie or stealing.

How can we argue with him? By pointing out the misery which he causes? If to point it out were the same thing as to make him feel it, the method might be successful; and we may hold that there is no reasonable being who has not, at least, the germs of sympathetic feeling, and therefore no one who is absolutely inaccessible to such appeals. But neither can we deny, without flying in the face of all experience, that in a vast number of cases the sympathies are so feeble and intermittent as to supply no motive capable of encountering the tremendous force of downright selfishness in a torpid nature. Shall we then appeal to some extrinsic motive—to the danger of being found out, despised, and punished? Undoubtedly, that will be effective as far as it goes. But if for any reason the man is beyond the reach of such dangers; if he is certain of escaping detection, or so certain that the chance of punishment does not outweigh the chance of impunity, he may despise our arguments, and we have no more to offer. . . . Against some people, in short, the only effective arguments are the gallows or the prison. Unluckily, they are arguments which cannot be brought to bear with all the readiness desirable, and therefore I think it highly probable that there will be bad men for a long time to come. . . . By acting rightly, I admit, even the virtuous man will sometimes be making a sacrifice; and I do not deny it to be a real sacrifice; I only deny that such a statement will be conclusive for the virtuous man. His own happiness is not his sole ultimate aim. . . . There is scarcely any man, I believe, at all capable of sympathy or reason (*sic*), who would not, in many cases unhesitatingly, sacrifice his own happiness for a sufficient advantage to others " (pp. 429, 431). In this passage the following points are worthy of notice: (1) That Mr. Stephen still lingers by the notion that happiness (though not necessarily the individual's) is the end. (2) That while it is true that the happiness of the individual and happiness of others normally coincide, yet they are different, and however near they come to one another, we can never be sure that they are one and will follow the same path. That which unites them in the good man " is sympathy," *i.e.*, a feeling. (3) Hence, to one who has not the feeling, there is no argument for unselfish adherence to the right which would appear conclusive. To which the reply is, " Of course not, if the connection between others' happiness and one's own is a feeling." You cannot tell a man he *ought* to have this feeling. It is sufficient that he has not got it.

"Ought," in fact, has disappeared from our vocabulary. But what if the end is not properly described as happiness, but as well-being or good; and the connection between individual and social good is not the subjective one of feeling, but, as Mr. Stephen inadvertently himself suggests, the objective one of " reason "?   Supposing that pleasure, whether egoistic or altruistic, is not his end, but that it is in virtue of his *being rational*, not in virtue of his *feeling sympathy*, that we appeal to a man to set aside selfish considerations, we are no longer left to seek for "arguments" to convince him that in following the " right " he is securing his own greatest happiness. We do not appeal to his sentient nature at all, but to his reason. It is on the ground of his being a rational self, incapable by his very nature of finding satisfaction in gratified feeling, that we are justified in setting aside all " arguments " founded on comparison of pleasures, and appealing directly to an "ought." Apart from this rational self, which can be shown to be essentially social, and therefore only capable of finding satisfaction in a *common good*, there can be no categorical imperative and no morality.

The form into which W. K. Clifford threw the evolutionist doctrine marks a stage of advance both upon Mr. Stephen's and upon Mr. Spencer's statement of it, in that he comes nearer than either to the view that right is founded upon the contrast between a true, or extended, and a false, or constricted self. In the following passage he applies his doctrine of " the tribal self " to solve a similar difficulty to that which Mr. Stephen discusses above. " ' If you want to live together in this complicated way ' (called society), ' your ways must be straight, and not crooked; you must seek the truth, and love no lie.' Suppose we answer, ' I don't want to live together with other men in this complicated way; and so I shall not do as you tell me,'— that is not the end of the matter, as it might be with other scientific precepts. For obvious reasons, it is *right* in this case to reply, ' Then, in the name of my people, I do not like you,' and to express this dislike by appropriate methods. And the offender, being descended from a social race, is unable to escape his conscience, the voice of his tribal self, which says, ' In the name of the tribe, I hate myself for this treason which I have done ' " (*Essays and Lectures*, " On the Scientific Basis of Morals "). We have here got beyond the pleasure theory; we have further exchanged the empirical for the teleological point of view, in so far as the "self" is made the centre of interest. All that is wanted is to ask what is implied in the idea of such a self. This, to a certain extent, Clifford does in his Essay on " Cosmic Emotion," where it is shown to imply a consciousness of a universal moral order. His early death probably lost us the opportunity of seeing evolutionary ethics discarding *in propria persona* the worn-out raiment of the empirical philosophy.

BOOK IV

THE END AS GOOD

CHAPTER I

§ 62. Summary of Results

WE may now sum up the results which our analysis and criticism have hitherto enabled us to reach :—(1) The standard of morality is primarily an end, not a law. Moral law is valid as flowing from the conception of a moral end, which cannot be mere obedience to law, whether supposed to be given by another or by self in the form of conscience. (2) The end is an ideal of self. As all voluntary action has some form of good for its aim, and all consciously conceived good may be described as realisation of self in one form or another, conduct which is judged to be absolutely, *i.e.*, morally, good is conduct whose end is the highest good, which again may be described as the realisation of the highest self. The *summum bonum* is to realise the *summus ego*. (3) The ideal self cannot be realised in the state of pleasant consciousness which results from the most complete satisfaction of the desire for pleasure; nor yet in the most complete determination by reason apart from all desire; but in the subordination of the desires according to the law of the self as an organic unity. (4). Finally, we have already made some headway, under the

151

lead of the evolutionist writers, in proving that the self as thus defined is not an isolated atom, but is only comprehensible as a member of a society, whose moral judgments reflect a moral order already established in its environment. But as the prejudice against the conception of the self as essentially social, and of moral judgments as only intelligible in relation to an objective moral order, is so inveterate, I shall devote part of this chapter to its further elucidation, as a preparation for the further definition of the end.

§ 63. Current Distinction between Self and Society

The current opinion * is that, while it requires a metaphysician like Hobbes to trace back all the elements and instincts of human nature to the egoistic desire for pleasure, it is yet possible to divide them psychologically into two distinct classes, the egoistic, or self-regarding, and the altruistic, or other-regarding. Of the former type we have the instinct of self-preservation and of the acquisition of property. Of the latter we have types in benevolence and sympathy. Similarly, there is the obvious social distinction beween man and the state, the individual and society. On the one hand, we have the "rights of man." The individual is supposed to be born into the world with certain natural rights belonging to him as an individual. These are the germ of that system of conventional or artificial rights with which in any civilised country the law courts invest him.† On

* Not unsupported by the highest scientific authorities, as when Mr. Spencer represents human nature as the battle-ground of two permanently antithetical forces of egoism and altruism.

† The natural rights of man apparently are liberty, property, security, and "Resistance of Oppression." See Declaration of the

the other hand, as securing to him the enjoyment of his natural rights by means of the police and the law courts, the state has a certain limited right of taxation and control over individuals. One of the chief questions for the political philosopher is, it is supposed, to define the limits which the state must observe in interfering with the natural rights of individuals. The quintessence of wisdom in this field is sometimes declared to be to recognise that, inasmuch as rights belong to man naturally and not in virtue of any connection with the artificial organisation of society and state, the state has really no business to interfere at all.

It is not difficult to show that these distinctions, though relatively valid, as giving us different points of view from which it may be useful to look at psychological and social facts, are misleading when taken as absolute and final.

§ 64. Relativity of these Distinctions

(1) *Egoistic and altruistic passions and desires.* Thus, in regard to the psychological distinctions referred to above between egoistic and altruistic desires, it is easy to show how the thought of self and the thought of others cross and interlace one another, in such a manner as to leave us with only a vanishing distinction between them. Thus, nothing seems more individual-

Rights of Man, quoted in Paine's treatise on the same. The Declaration of Rights in the Constitution of the State of California further adds the right of "pursuing and obtaining (!) happiness." See Bryce's *American Commonwealth*, Vol. II., p. 643. As necessary corollaries of these some add "access to the soil"; others, more generally, "access to the means of production."

istic than the desire for *life*. But the moment we think of it, we see how in a rational being it is its social significance that makes life valuable to him. It is doubtful whether in a moment of peril a normally constituted individual thinks first, or even at all, of himself, except so far as he is related to others. His thoughts fly, *e.g.*, to his wife and family. When life is emptied of these relations, *i.e.*, when it appears only as an egoistic good, it is no good at all. It is just its emptiness of social content that makes life appear so worthless to the suicide.

On the other hand, the benevolent desire for the good of others involves a reference to self. By this it is not merely meant, as Professor Bain puts it, that "sympathy cannot exist upon the extreme of self-abnegation. . . . We must retain a sufficient amount of the self-regarding element to consider happiness an object worth striving for," * but that, as has been already so frequently pointed out, the object of all desire is a personal good. Hence it is only as involved in one's own that one can desire one's neighbour's good: it is only as his good enters as an element into *my* conception of *my* good that I can make it an object of desire and volition.

The inadequacy of such a classification of the elements of human nature into egoistic and altruistic is further seen in the difficulty which we should have in classifying the more violent forms of passion under either head. Thus love in its purer forms is commonly thought to be an altruistic emotion, having for its object the good of the loved object. Yet it may on occasions take forms into which the good of the loved object does not enter as an

---

* *Mental and Moral Science*, p. 282.

element.* Similarly revenge, which is presumably upon this classification to be set down as an egoistic passion, nevertheless takes forms which involve the most complete self-abnegation.†

(2) *The Individual and Society.* In regard to the relations of the individual to society, it may likewise be shown that the independent rights put forward on behalf of the individual, by current individualistic theories, are, if taken literally, an arbitrary assumption. Whence, it may be asked, does the individual derive them? He has them, it may be said, by *nature* (the theory of "natural rights" seems to imply this). "Man," said Rousseau, "is born free," *i.e.,* independent of the laws, habits, and conventions of society. But this is certainly not the case. The child who comes into the world inherits everything he has from a previous state of society. He owes everything he possesses to a combination of forces and circumstances (national, local, and family influences) over which he has had no control. It was a favourite metaphor with the older individualistic writers to liken the soul of the newly born child to a piece of blank paper, on which, by means of education, anything might be written, and so a

---

* In describing Romola's love for her dead father, G. Eliot says: "Love does not aim simply at the conscious good of the beloved object: it is not satisfied without perfect loyalty of heart; it aims at its own completeness."

† Speaking of the passion that consumes Baldassare in the same novel, G. Eliot says: "It is the nature of all human passion, the lowest as well as the highest, that there is a point where it ceases to be properly egoistic, and is like a fire kindled within our being, to which everything else in us is mere fuel." Similarly hatred has been defined as "inverted love"; it is often like love in this, that "it seeketh not its own."

perfectly independent and original character given to the
individual. It would be a more apt illustration of its
true nature to compare it to a word or sentence in a
continuous narrative. The soul comes into the world
already stamped with a meaning determined by its
relation to all that went before,—having, in other words,
a context in relation to which alone its character can be
understood. It sums up the tendencies and traditions
of the past out of which it has sprung,—giving them,
indeed, a new form or expression, inasmuch as it is an
individual, but only carrying on and developing their
meaning, and not to be understood except in relation to
them.

Or it may be said that man acquires these rights by
education. Knowledge gives him power, individuality,
freedom. This, of course, is true, but not in the sense
that with these advantages he acquires any rights as
against society. On the contrary, the dependence of
the individual upon society in the sense claimed is still
more obvious when we consider what is implied in
education. Thus it may be pointed out how absurd it
is to speak, as is sometimes done, of a "self-educated
man." No one can be said, in any proper sense, to
educate himself. Nor indeed can any individual properly
be said to gain his education from another. Parent
or teacher can only help to open and interpret to
him the sources of education. That education has
begun long before it is consciously thought of, and
goes on long after it is supposed to be completed.
Intellectually it consists from first to last in the appropriation of a body of knowledge, not contained in the
mind of any individual parent or teacher, but diffused
through the language and literature of the society

into which the child is born. The child has not
to make its own ideas about the world, nor has the
parent or teacher to make them for it. In spoken
language, which is essentially a social institution,* there
is already a store-house of distinctions and generalisations which the child begins by appropriating. Its
thoughts adapt themselves to the mould which is here
prepared for them. They will be accurate and adequate
in proportion (*a*) to the stage of accuracy which the
language has reached (*i.e.*, the stage of intellectual
advance which the society whose language it is represents); (*b*) to the degree of culture which the group of
persons who form its immediate society have attained.
Not less representative of social acquisitions is the written language of books. This or that man indeed is said
to write a book : he puts his name at the beginning of it,
and his list of authorities in the preface or at the end.
But in most cases it would represent the fact more accurately if he put the names of his authorities on the title
page, and stowed away his own in some obscurer corner.
All that he has done, all that he can do, is to recast the
material supplied him by the labour of countless generations. His book is at best only a clever compilation
from these.†

The same remarks apply to the child's moral education.
Here, again, it is not we who educate our children, but
language with its store of ready-made moral distinctions,
the nursery with its "spirit," its laws, and, as Plato
would add, its pictures and songs, the family, the play-

---

* The Emperor Augustus confessed that, with all his power, he
was unable to make a new word.

† Hence Emerson accuses every one of being a plagiarist.
Everything, he says, is a plagiarism,—" a *house* is a plagiarism."

ground, and the church. These begin to act upon the child's moral life, forming or deforming it, at a time when direct verbal instruction is impossible. From its earliest infancy, to use a philosopher's somewhat grandiloquent expression, the child "has been suckled at the breast of the Universal Ethos."*

§ 65. Further Illustrations of Dependence of Individual on Society

In industry this truth has a still more obvious application. Thus we sometimes hear in business of a "self-made man." But a moment's consideration makes it obvious that it is as impossible for a man to "make" himself as we saw it to be for him to educate himself. All he does is to use the opportunities that society offers to him. Where, to look no further, would his factory or business be but for the police who protect it, the laws that secure him the title deeds, the markets that supply the raw material, the community that supplies the labour to work it, the system of railways, harbours, etc., that are the means of disposing of the product? What is the share that all these things, each in its turn depending for its existence and efficiency upon a community of organised wills, as well as on the social labour of many generations, have in the wealth that is produced, and what is the share of the energetic individual who uses them? where in all this are we to draw the line between the respective rights of the man and of the state?

As a final illustration, we might take the case of great men. These, at any rate, it might be thought, are an exception to this dependence of the individual upon

* On the subject of this section, see Bradley, *op. cit.*, pp. 145-58.

his society and his time. They stand out in solitary independence of the society in the midst of which they live. If they have not made themselves, they seem to have been made by God, and to owe little or nothing to their environment. Cæsar, Charlemagne, Napoleon, may thus be proved to have been makers of their social environment, instead of having been made by it. And indeed there is a sense in which this is true. Such men seem to contribute a new element to social progress, and to leave the world different from what they found it. But when we look closer we see that they do so, not in virtue of that which separates them from their time, but of that which unites them to it. It is their insight into the wants of the time, their sympathy with its blind longings and aspirations, that gives them their power over it. They are closer to the spirit of the time, and the moral order which that spirit represents, not further away from it, than common people. This is the secret of their greatness. It is on this account that they "represent" their time.* They sum up and give expression to its tendencies. It is not so much they who act, as the spirit of the time that acts in them. The permanent part of their work (the establishment of an empire, of a system of education, or a new social organisation) was "in the air" when the man arrived. He was only an instrument in giving effect to it.

§ 66. Ethical Import of These Facts

(1) The first consequence of the truth I have been illustrating which it is of importance for us to note is that the end which is the standard of moral judgment

* *Cp.* Ben Jonson's apostrophe to Shakespeare as " Soul of the Age."

is a social one—the good is common good. A being
who, like man, is a little higher than the animals, "a little
lower than the angels," can only realise his own life in
so far as he realises the life of the society of which he
is a member.* To maintain himself in isolated independence, to refuse to be compromised by social relations,
is the surest way to fail to realise the good he seeks.† To
seek life in this sense is to lose it. On the other hand,
a man finds salvation in the duties of family, profession,
city, country. To lose his life in these is to find it. For
the social fabric of which he finds himself a part is only
the fabric of his own life "writ large." It is only the
other, or objective side, of that which subjectively I
described as the system of his impulses and desires, as
controlled and organised by his reason. It might seem,
at first sight, an illustration of an *ignotum per ignotius* to
refer us from the desires and impulses, which we know
as parts of ourselves, to the vague field of social rights
and duties, which appeal to us only in a secondary way
through moral rules and social conventions, were it
not for the knack that these rights and duties have of
grouping themselves in visible institutions. Thus, corresponding to the instinct of self-preservation and the
rights and duties it involves, civilisation has produced
the police and law courts; corresponding to the instinct
of propagation, the family; of acquisition, property and
trade; of the pursuit of truth, the school, university, and

---

* Aristotle said that one who is independent of society is either
"a god or a beast."

† As a simple illustration of this truth, I may quote the case of a
man whose vote I once solicited for one of several strongly opposed
candidates for the School Board. His answer was that he was an
independent man, and intended to prove it by not voting at all.

academy of science. Apart from these, and the rights
and duties they represent, the individual life shrivels up
into quite insignificant proportions;* in connection with
them it expands to the full extent of its recognised
capabilities.

The same truth might be illustrated from the side of
vice and evil. As the good of the individual is the
common good, so his evil is common evil. No one can
neglect the duty he owes himself of findng the equilibrium
of his instincts and desires in the due proportion of their
exercise, without failing in his duty to society, and dis-
turbing the equilibrium of functions which constitute its
health and well-being. The man who drinks away his
wages, and upsets the equilibrium between desire for
drink and desire for health, if he fails of no duty nearer
home, deprives his trade or profession of an efficient
member, and so is a source of common loss and evil.
And just as we have the wholesome institutions of family,
trade, the universities, etc., corresponding to the har-
monious and proportionate satisfaction of natural instincts, so, corresponding to disorganisation in the system
of desires, we have the morbid growth of brothels, gam-
bling dens, cribs, and cramming establishments.†

(2) It is only expressing the same truth in a more
particular form to point out that the self is not merely
related to society in general, but that each particular self
is related in a special way to the society into which he is

---

* Becoming, as Hobbes puts it, "solitary, poor, nasty, brutish,
short."

† It is common to make a distinction between sins of omission
and commission. If the above account is true, this is merely superficial. To omit a duty is as much a common evil as to commit a
positive trespass.

born. This way is best described under the form, which is not an ingenious metaphor, but a vital fact, of membership. The individual is not less vitally related to society than the hand or the foot to the body. Nor is it merely that each individual is dependent for life and protection upon society, as the hand or the foot is dependent for its nourishment upon the body, but he is dependent on his particular relation to society for the particular form of his individuality. It is the function it performs in virtue of its special place in the organism which makes the hand a hand, and the foot a foot. In the same way it is his place and function in society that makes the in‐dividual what he is. He realises himself by enabling society, through him, to perform the particular function which is represented by his station and its duties.*

§ 67. Appeal to Moral Judgments in support of Conclusions

We have thus arrived at a new statement of the nature of the self, which, as the standard of moral judgment, I formerly described as the permanent unity underlying the multiplicity of desire. This, which may

---

* See Bradley, *op. cit.*, pp. 157-86. *Cp. Essays in Philosophical Criticism* (Ed. Seth and R. B. Haldame), "The Social Organism," by Professor Henry Jones, esp. pp. 193, 209 foll. Dewey points out that (1) the fulfilment of the duties of one's station, or, as he calls it, "adjustment to environment," can be taken as a moral ideal only on condition that it means "willing the maintenance and development of moral surroundings as one's own end "; (2) The function that is thus performed serves at once to define and to unite. It makes a man "a *distinct* social member at the same time that it makes him a *member.* . . . Individuality means, not separation, but defined position in a whole " (*op. cit.*, pp. 115 foll., 137, 138).

have appeared a somewhat metaphysical statement, I am now able to translate into the familiar language of every-day life, in so far as I have shown that this unity amid diversity assumes visible form in that circle of inter-related duties which we call a man's station in society. It remains merely to verify this explanation of moral judgments by submitting it to the test of fact, and asking whether moral judgments, which we have seen involve a reference to a true self or rational order among instincts and desires, bear out the interpretation I have just given to that self as essentially social by carrying with them a reference to a society or objective moral order as well.

That this is so with regard to a large section of our moral judgments is obvious. Injustice, dishonesty, untruthfulness, covetousness, are all judged bad on the ground of the harm to others they involve. So fully has this been recognised, that it has sometimes been proposed to resolve all virtue into right relations with our fellow-men under the common name of Justice, Benevolence, or Truth. But it is not so clear that this social reference is universally present in moral judgments, when we come to consider the so-called individualistic virtues and the duties we are said to owe to ourselves.

In the next chapter I shall have occasion to remark in detail how these involve a social reference. Here it will be sufficient to take what is regarded as the first duty we owe to ourselves, the duty of self-preservation. And that it may not be obscured by obvious reference to "social ties," which may in a particular instance "bind a man to life," such as his duty to his wife and family, we must suppose all these ties have been dis-

solved, and life to have been to all appearance emptied
of social significance. What, it may be asked, is implied
in our judgment that suicide is wrong in such a case?
Ex hypothesi there are no relations that can have any
claim upon the would-be suicide. He is without
friends, money, trade, or the hope of acquiring them.
Here, if anywhere, it might be supposed our judgment
refers to the individual. In parting with his life, he is
merely parting with his own. If there is a duty in the
matter, it is merely a duty to himself. There is no duty
to society, and therefore society has no right to interfere
with what is strictly his own affair.*

To all this society in most civilised countries, as
is well known, replies, rudely enough, with the police-
man's baton, the prison, or the lunatic asylum. It
may indeed be said that this is no sufficient answer
to the claim that is put forward. For the State may
be wrong. Its judgments in this matter may not
be in conformity with any true standard of right. But
we have already seen reason in the nature of man
himself for believing that its interference in this case
is not without ethical justification. For if what was
said in the earlier part of this chapter be sound, no man
has a right to take his own life, because no man has a life
of his own to take. His life has been given him, and has
been made all that it is, as has been already shown, by
society. He cannot morally part with it without consent
of a society which is joint-owner with him in it. He

---

* This, of course, is constantly urged in defence of suicide; and if
we take up the position that certain duties rest on the value which
life has to the individual alone, it is difficult to see what answer
there can be. Hence individualistic theories of ethics, *e.g.*, Stoicism,
have always tended to justify suicide.

carries on his life as a joint concern: he cannot dissolve the partnership without the consent of his partner in it.* Perhaps in the case selected society may have shamefully neglected its part. So far society is wrong, and is responsible for the state to which matters have come, but this does not absolve the individual from his duty to society. Two wrongs do not make a right.

§ 68.   Duty to Humanity

Nor do we alter the social implication of moral judgment by saying that the duty in such cases is not to the state or community to which he belongs, but to God or to humanity, for this only brings into view a wider aspect of the moral order than that which we have hitherto considered. Thus, to take the latter contention first, to speak of our interest in humanity as the ground of obligation is only to extend our conception of what is implied in the moral order which we call society. It is to conceive of it as reaching beyond the limits of any particular

* *Cp.* Burke's famous description: " Society is indeed a contract. Subordinate contracts for objects of mere occasional interest may be dissolved at pleasure; but the state ought not to be considered as nothing better than a partnership agreement in a trade of pepper and coffee, calico or tobacco, or some other such low concern, to be taken up for a little temporary interest, and to be dissolved by the fancy of the parties. It is to be looked on with other reverence; because it is not a partnership subservient only to the gross animal existence of a temporary and perishable nature. It is a partnership in all science, a partnership in all art, a partnership in every virtue and in all perfection. As the ends of such a partnership cannot be obtained in many generations, it becomes a partnership not only between those who are living, but between those who are living, those who are dead, and those who are to be born."—*Reflections on the Revolution in France.*

time and country, and as progressively realising itself
over the whole world and through the ages. The existence of such an order is not doubted by the historian.
History, in the ordinary sense, is the record of the form
which it takes, and the changes it undergoes, in a particular age or country. Universal history is the record
of these forms and changes as organically related to one
another, and to the whole which we call the growth or
evolution of civilisation.*

Loyalty to the moral order in this sense is involved in
loyalty to the narrower circle of duties which represent
it for the individual. On the other hand, the former is
impossible apart from the latter. It is not possible to
do our duty to humanity, and leave undone our duty
to our neighbour. Dickens has made us laugh over
Mrs. Jellyby's "telescopic philanthropy." But in his
humorous description of that lady's humanitarian ec-
centricities the novelist is only emphasising the truth
which the philosopher expresses in different language
when he reminds us that "there is no other genuine enthusiasm for humanity than one which has travelled the
common highway of reason—the life of the good neighbour and the honest citizen—and can never forget that it
is still only a further stage of the same journey." †

§ 69. Duty to God

In the same way it may be shown that to speak of the
duties in question as owed to God and not to society is

---

* For a sketch of history in this sense, see Hegel's *Philosophy of History* (Bohn's Library).

† T. H. Green's *Introd. to the Moral Part of Hume's "Treatise,"* Works, Vol. I., p. 371.

a perfectly legitimate mode of expression so long as we understand what we mean by it. Thus, it cannot be meant that in using it we are introducing a new conception of the ground of obligation. It cannot be too often repeated that the ground of moral obligation is always a personal interest in a moral order. It may, however, be legitimate to express this truth in the language of religion as well as of ethics. In the latter we confine our view to the moral order which is represented by particular societies, or by humanity as a whole. But it is possible to extend our view still further, and to conceive of the establishment of moral relations and the sovereignty of conscience as elements in the end or final cause of a cosmic process. In doing so we pass from the point of view of morality to that of religion, but no further change is involved. It is indeed sometimes supposed that there are religious duties which are not included in the catalogue of moral duties, and that in passing from morality to religion we not only change the point of view from which duties are regarded, but extend the range of our obligations. But this is a mistake. The particulars of conduct, not less than the ground of obligation, are the same whether we speak of duty to society or duty to God. It is indeed true that the religious man may recognise duties which others deny or neglect. Of these prayer, fasting, and other ceremonial observances may be quoted as instances. But it ought to be observed that it is the import of these rites for morality which gives them their importance for religion. If this import be recognised by the individual; if it be acknowledged, for instance, that they serve an important end in purifying the affections or capturing the will,* they are not only religiously but morally obligatory. Apart from such recognition, not only are they irrelevant to the moral, and therefore to the religious life, they may be an actual hindrance to both.

Is there then no difference, it might be asked, between religion and morality? Matthew Arnold, as is well known, sought to answer this question in his famous definition of the former as only "morality touched with emotion." But this, it must be confessed, does not carry us far. Emotion is not a distinctive mark of religious conduct. All conduct, as we have already seen, is touched with emotion,† otherwise it would not be conduct at all. The distinction lies not in the presence of an element of emotion in religion which morality is without, but in the *kind* of emotion present in either case, and this again depends on the kind of *thought* which accompanies the performance of a duty. It is the way we think of the duty, the view we take of it, that constitutes it simply moral or also religious. Thus, to return to the class of duties from which we started, an act of self-restraint or self-preservation might be said to be simply moral if it were done out of sympathy with the lives and purposes of a special group of our fellow-creatures, without further reference to what is implied in such a fellowship. The same act would be religious if it were conceived of as furthering a cosmic purpose, or as charged with meaning for a universal moral order that is being consummated upon the earth. It may indeed be feasibly maintained that no good conduct is entirely without reference to

---

* *Cp.* Pascal's pious exhortation "to begin by sprinkling holy water and observing ceremonies," for that "*the rest would follow*," and Höffding's remarks upon it, *Psychology* (Eng. Tr.), p. 76.

† See analysis of Desire, p. 46.

some such universal end; but in so far as the distinction
between morality and religion is permissible at all, it
must be explained as one between two views that may
be taken of moral conduct, not between two different
kinds of conduct, or two different standards of moral
judgment.

CHAPTER II

FORMS OF THE GOOD

§ 70. Recapitulation

In looking for the basis of moral judgment, we were led
to the conclusion that it must be sought in the idea of
an end, which, as the end of conduct, must be an end
for *me*. With these "data of ethics"—viz. (*a*) moral
judgments of right and wrong, good and bad; (*b*) as involved in these, the conception of an end; and (*c*) the
definition of the end as a form of self-satisfaction, or, as
we preferred to say, self-realisation—we approached the
criticism of theories as to the nature of the end. We
first took up the older theories, which represent the end
respectively as pleasure and self-sacrifice. The defect
of these theories was not that they start from a conception of the self, and recognise moral judgment as based
upon it; but that they start from the wrong conception
of it,—with the result that, instead of explaining moral
judgment, they in reality explain it away. Hedonism
does so by identifying the right and the expedient, and
thus failing to explain how an "ought" or a categorical
imperative can exist at all. Equally defective is the

theory that the end is the sacrifice of all desire. For,
apart from desire, there can be no action; so that
the theory not only fails to account for moral judgment,
but leaves no place in a strictly moral world for the eager
passions and desires which are the life-blood of common
life. The concrete life of social activity, as founded on
desires for the good of ourselves and others, disappears
on this theory altogether.

Both theories, while thus differing in their conception
of the self, agree in being individualistic. If we represent the problem they had to solve as that of finding the
link of connection between moral judgments and the
maxims of conduct which flow from them on the one
hand, and the *summum bonum* on the other, we might
say that they were both right in perceiving that the
middle term, through which the solution was to be
accomplished, was the self. The error, however, which
made the problem insoluble for both, was that they conceived of the self in an abstract way, apart from its social
relations, and thus robbed it of the content which might
have given us the desired connection.

Our objection to evolutionary ethics was different.
We gladly accepted from it the organic conception of
the relation between the individual and society. We objected merely to the way in which this idea was applied
in ethics. After dropping the individualistic theory,
we should have expected the writers in question to go
on to a more thorough-going examination of the conception of self, which we saw to be the basis of moral
judgment. Instead of this, they have allowed themselves
to drift away from the idea of personal good altogether,
and have attempted to work out a teleological science,
or a science of consciously conceived ends, as though its

object were the conflict of emotional forces empirically given.*

In the last chapter we endeavoured to put ourselves right in this last respect, by showing that the self is only intelligible as the reflection of a moral order, which, for practical purposes, we found might be considered as represented to each of us by his station and his duties, so that "the good" for each comes to be expressible in terms of his social relations—in other words, of good conduct itself.

It is not pretended that this is more than a rough statement of the end or standard of moral judgment. Some of the modifications and corrections which further consideration renders necessary will be the subject of the following book. Meantime, I shall try to give greater definiteness to it by considering some of the chief forms of the good, which, as I have shown, will merely be forms of good conduct. But, before doing so, I must endeavour to meet an objection which is sure to occur at this point in our argument.

§ 71. Has my Argument been a Circle?

Has not my argument, it may be asked, though developed with all the appearance of consecutive reasoning, only succeeded after all in involving us in a circle? I started out to *explain* moral judgments, in the sense of deducing them from an end to which they should be seen to be organically related. I then defined the end as realisation of self; and finally, to the question, "How is the self realised?" I replied, on behalf of the average

---

* See the celebrated chapters (xi.-xiv.), in Spencer's *Data of Ethics*, on Egoism *versus* Altruism.

man, " By loyalty to the ordinary duties of the good parent
and honest citizen." Starting from good conduct, and
professing to explain what this is through the idea of
end, I have finished up by defining the end in terms
of good conduct. We thus seem, like the heroes of the
song, to have merely "marched up the hill, and then
marched down again." We have ascended from the
idea of good conduct to the idea of end, only to descend
again to the idea of good conduct, and are no further on
than we were at the beginning.

My first answer is: Granting it to be a circle, it may
be none the worse for that. No one complains of the
guide who takes him up the mountain that he takes him
back to the starting-point. The journey may have been
of value, though he returns at the end of it to the same
place. As a matter of fact, the same traveller never does
return to the same place. He is "a different man " when
he comes back, and the home he comes back to is a
"different place." In the same way, it is possible that
the reader who has followed this argument may seem
to have come back to the point from which he started;
but he may have seen a good deal by the way, and may
really have come back (as the writer hopes he has) with
a quite different idea of what good conduct really is;
i.e., he may have come back to quite a different point.

But the objection is in reality founded on a false view of
the nature of the moral end. It proceeds on the assumption that the end in reference to which conduct is judged
to have value, the ideal which good conduct aims at
realising, is something *to be attained in the long run*.
The end of man, as man, is conceived of as the end of
the artist would be. It is something to be produced by
a series of actions, each leading up to a final result, and

standing to it in the relation of means to end. The
Greeks were not slow to perceive the fallacy of this
notion, and at the beginning of his treatise on ethics
Aristotle * is careful to point out that the end for man,
as man, is attained in the action itself. It is conduct
($\pi\rho\hat{a}\xi\iota\varsigma$ = Lat. *actio*), not production ($\pi o\acute{\iota}\eta\sigma\iota\varsigma$ = Lat.
factio). Similarly Christianity recognised that "the
kingdom of heaven is within you." Expressed in modern
language, this means that the end or ideal in morals is
not to be conceived of as "some far-off divine event"
which is some day to come to pass. It is daily and
hourly realised in the good act itself. Such an act is
not a means to a further end: it is itself the end. In its
completeness (the purity of its motive, the beneficence
of its results) the end *is* realised. The good is not
something to be hereafter attained: it is attained from
moment to moment in the good life itself. Hence
some † have been content to define the good as the
good will, by which is meant, not a will which acts
independently of desire, but the will which in the
indulgence of the particular desires that from moment
to moment form the undercurrent of our daily lives is
habitually determined by a more or less consciously
conceived idea of a *person* whose satisfaction is only to
be found in a certain order of their mutual subordination.
The truth intended to be emphasised by this mode of
expression is the truth that satisfaction does not exist
somewhere, laid up in store for the future, but must be
realised in the good action itself; and that the moral end
is *sui generis* in this, that the distinction of end and

---

* *Ethics*, I., I.

† *E.g.*, Kant and T. H. Green, who held that "the only uncon-
ditioned good is the good will."

means is a distinction within itself,—in other words, has no proper place as a distinction here at all. We may, therefore, have no further hesitation in defining the forms of good, or modes of self-realisation, as forms of good conduct, and *vice versâ*.

§ 72. Virtues and Institutions

The previous discussion has prepared us for a double classification of the duties or forms of good conduct. These may be classified according to the virtues or qualities of character which lead to their recognition, or to the social institutions which guarantee a field for their exercise.   In the former they are considered subjectively as habits of will; in the latter objectively as the sphere in which the good will realises itself.   It has been maintained * that the latter is the true classification, inasmuch as moral institutions provide us with a ready-made map of the different parts of the moral life. They are "the mode in which morality gives effect to the various wants of mankind."   But it has to be observed that, as we have seen, there is corresponding to the system of objective institutions a subjective system of impulses and desires, and that the virtues or aptitudes (ἀρεταί) for restraining and co-ordinating natural instincts, and so giving effect to the self as an organic whole, are just as natural a basis of classification as are the institu-

---

* As by Mr. Alexander, *op. cit.*, p. 253. Though I have criticised one or two minor points in Mr. Alexander's remarks on the subject of this chapter, what he says on it is so valuable that the student is recommended to read the passage referred to in connection with what follows. On the general subject of this section, see Dewey, *op. cit.*, pp. 169-74.

tions which are maintained by means of them. It is doubtful, moreover, whether in actual fact the difficulties which are admitted to exist in any attempt at an exhaustive classification are not felt equally in connection with the one system as with the other. Granted, as is indeed true in a general sense, that duties "naturally attach to the institutions, and are defined by them," it would yet be difficult to say round what institutions more than others the duties, *e.g.*, of courage, veracity, toleration naturally group themselves.

As a matter of fact, a complete system of ethics would require to exhibit the forms of good under both aspects, as related on the one side to the system of instincts and desires known as human nature, and on the other to the objective moral order, as that is embodied in social institutions. In the one case we should be supplementing our exposition of the principles of ethics by a more or less elaborate psychological account of the springs of action.* In the other case we should be adding to the science of ethics in the stricter sense a sociological account of the principal forms which man, in his efforts after a fuller expression of his true nature, has devised to be the repositories of his moral acquisitions.† In this handbook neither of these is attempted. Following the guidance of common language, I have adopted, with slight modifications, a classification of the virtues in its main lines as old as Aristotle, merely with the view of

---

* For such an account see, *e.g.*, Martineau's *Types of Ethical Theory*, Vol. II., pp. 128 foll.

† It is characteristic of German as contrasted with English ethics to have emphasised this side of the moral life. Perhaps this is natural where the state counts for so much and the individual for so little.

showing how actual moral duties, and the judgments that correspond to them, flow from the conception of the self as set forth above.*

§ 73. Requirements in such a Classification

(1) To be of any use for our purpose, as thus defined, the classification must neither be too general nor run into too great detail. Thus Plato's celebrated classification of the virtues into Wisdom, Courage, Temperance, Justice, is obviously too meagre, and, as has been well said, "serves its purpose only because justice is used to include everything not accounted for by the rest." On

---

* Virtue has been used in the preceding paragraph in its proper sense of the quality of character that fits for the discharge of duty. In this sense it is not opposed to duty, save as good character in general is opposed to good conduct in general. The relation between virtue and duty is that of universal to particular, and may be illustrated by the relation of the state to the individual. The character of a man's action, in reference to particular circumstances, is determined by the virtuous habit of will with reference to the particular form of desire that is called into exercise, just as the character of an individual citizen is determined by the character of the society to which he belongs. The performance of the duty has moral quality only in so far as it is the expression of a virtue; virtue, on the other hand, only lives in the performance of duty. It should be pointed out, however, that the word is often loosely used in the sense of meritorious act, as when we speak of "making a virtue of necessity." Here it is distinguished from duty, as the meritorious act is distinguished from the act which is simply good: the meritorious act being that which is the result of a higher than the average standard of virtue, whether in overcoming natural disadvantages, as when we speak of the diligence of a stupid scholar as meritorious, or in achieving exceptional success *ceteris paribus*. On the distinction between virtue and duty, see Sidgwick's *Methods of Ethics*, Book III., ch. ii., and on the subject of the succeeding sections, *ibid.*, chs. iii.-x.

the other hand, if, as has been shown to be the case, virtue has to do with the regulation of the instincts and desires, the list of which is practically inexhaustible,* its forms will be legion. Language, fortunately, prescribes for us the mean in these two directions. It indicates a sufficient variety of moral distinctions, but makes no attempt to cover the whole field by having words for all the possible virtues. In many cases, it is content with general names, under which whole classes are brought. Thus *self-control* is the general word for the regulation of the desire for pleasure; *courage*, of the desire to escape from pain. But of these desires there are many varieties, according to the nature of the object desired or feared (according as the object of desire is the pleasure of eating or of drinking, of seeing or of learning, etc., the object of fear—physical or mental, near or distant, short or prolonged pain). Language has here picked out a few prominent instances, as in connecting *temperance* with the regulation of the desire for strong drink, *endurance* with the regulation of the impulse to escape or mitigate continued pain.

(2) A second obvious requirement for our purpose is, that the division should follow the main outline of the organic parts or relations of the self. Only in this way shall we be dividing our subject as Plato required we should—"at the joints."

Hence such grounds of distinction as that between determinate and indeterminate duties, or duties of perfect and duties of imperfect obligation, will be useless to us. For by this it is meant that some duties are defi-

---

* For an interesting fragment of such a list, see William James's *Principles of Psychology*, Vol. II., ch. xxiv. *Cp.* p. 43 *n.* above.

nitely determined by law or custom, while others are left
to the discretion of the individual. Of the former the
duty to pay one's debts is a familiar example; of the
latter, the duty of charity. But such a principle of
classification is misleading. There is an element of
indeterminateness in all duty, inasmuch as the precise
form that the duty takes must depend in each case upon
the circumstances. It is quite true that it is a determinate duty to pay one's debts; but the time, the place,
the manner, frequently the amount, are matters left
indeterminate. On the other hand, all duty which is
duty at all is a "bounden" duty. If it is a duty to be
charitable, it is of as perfect obligation as any other. In
this sense an indeterminate duty, or a duty of imperfect
obligation, is a contradiction in terms.

Again, it is proposed to divide virtues according to
their importance, beginning with the "cardinal virtues,"
and going down through all degrees until we come to
the lesser duties of social etiquette and politeness. The
difficulty in this case is, that the relative importance of
the virtues varies, not only from age to age in the history
of the world, but from class to class in any one community, and even from individual to individual. Thus
it has been well observed that each age has had its
cardinal (or papal) virtue. Among the Greeks and
Romans it was courage, or manliness (ἀρετή, *virtus*);
among the early Christians it was charity: in the middle ages, chivalry; in the eighteenth century, benevolence; to-day, perhaps, it is what Mr. Leslie Stephen
calls "organic justice." Similarly, in different classes
in a community virtues vary in importance. Courage is
more important in a soldier than in a tailor, truthfulness
and sincerity in a clergyman than in a lawyer, toleration

in a ruler than in a subject. Lastly, in the life of the
individual, the circumstances of his own temptations, or
the importance of his example, may make a particular
virtue (*e.g.*, temperance) the cardinal one for him, while
for another it may be different.

§ 74. Limits of Classification. The Main Heads not mutually Exclusive

Before going on to suggest a classification which may
in some degree satisfy these requirements, it may be
well to recall some of the results arrived at in the previous investigation, that we may know in what sense
such a classification is really possible.

(1) In the first place, we may remind ourselves
that the self, of whose moral qualities we are attempting a general description, is not an aggregate of parts
mechanically put together, and mutually exclusive of one
another. Each part is organically related to every other:
each therefore implies the other, as well as the whole
through which it is united to it. Thus, reason implies
will, as the student may observe for himself if he pauses
to note how much voluntary effort has been required in
the act of comprehending the argument in the present
chapter. Similarly will implies reason, while each is only
comprehensible as a different aspect of one subject that
embraces both.* Hence, when in the common classification it is proposed to draw a distinction between
intellectual and moral virtues,—or Wisdom and Virtue
proper,—we shall know in what sense to accept the
division. It cannot mean that these exclude one
another, or that we are here doing more than dis-

* See Green, *op. cit.*, Book II., ch. ii., §§ 148 foll.

tinguishing between elements or aspects of all morality.
In the case of the former, it is undoubtedly true that
we are dealing primarily with the relations of things
or events to one another in an objective world of
fact; in the case of the latter we are dealing primarily
with relations of persons to one another. But it is
not difficult to show that the virtues implied in right
dealing in each of these spheres, involve each other.
Thus, in reference to the self-regarding virtues, it hardly
requires to be stated that they involve an element of
wisdom. The common description of them as "prudential" implies this. Even proverbial philosophy
teaches us that "*discretion* is the better part of valour."
It might have added the converse, that valour is the
better part of wisdom or discretion, for it is equally
true that—

> " He wants wit who wants *resolved will*
>   To learn his wit to exchange the bad for better."

It is hardly less obvious that the other-regarding virtues of justice * and benevolence presuppose knowledge
(*c.g.*, of economic and physical laws), while, on the
other hand, it may be doubted whether the pursuit of
truth,† divorced from sympathy with social needs and
aspirations, has any claim to be called a virtue.

(2) If again we recall the truth on which so much
has been said, that self and society are related to one
another as particular and universal, and are therefore
only different sides of the one reality, we shall be
prepared to estimate the common distinction between

---

* Who, as she is commonly depicted, is *blinded*, not *blind*.

† The same is true, of course, of beauty. *Cp.* Note at the end of
this chapter.

self-regarding and other-regarding virtues at its proper value. We shall be ready to admit that these are aspects of the same habit or quality of mind. Prudence and self-control are the necessary conditions of justice and benevolence. On the other hand, that which gives prudence and self-control a claim to be called virtues is the fact that they are the indispensable condition of all social service from the lowest to the highest.

§ 75. The Interdependence of the Virtues extends through the Whole Classification

But we cannot stop here. The interdependence which we find to exist between the several highest species in our classification of the *summum genus* Virtue, may be expected to prevail also among the lower species of which these in turn are general. If, as we have assumed throughout, human nature is an organic whole, and not merely an aggregate of parts, we may expect to find it equally impossible to treat the special virtues, each of which, in its separate department, is the guarantee of its unity, as independent units. Hence it is an error to distinguish, as some have sought to do, between the main heads of morality, such as wisdom and self-control, and the other virtues, on the ground that they do not correspond to any special groups of duties or observances, but are implied in all good actions. It is certainly true that on any classification these would require to be treated as *summae species*, and as such might be considered generalised expressions for the various species which in turn should be subsumed under them. But this must not be interpreted to mean that there is

any greater independence among the lower species than
among the higher. There is, of course, a greater
differentiation as we descend, and the relationships of
the various parts to one another are accordingly more
remote; but to press this distinction, so as to divide
aspects or elements of virtue from virtues proper, is to
deny the organic nature of virtue itself. It is as though
in classifying the muscles of any organic body we were
to begin by separating off the respiratory, alimentary,
reproductive, and other systems, and, after baptising them
"aspects of the muscular system as a whole," were to
refuse them a place in a continuous classification along
with the muscles of the special organs in each several
group.

It is, in fact, as impossible to draw hard and fast lines
between the virtues (*e.g.*, of courage and temperance,
which are species of self-control, or between devotion to
truth in knowledge and veracity in society, which are
species of intellectual virtue) as it is to draw a hard and
fast line between self-control and wisdom themselves. It
is just as open to us to speak of these sub-species as elements or aspects of self-control or wisdom, as to speak of
self-control and wisdom as aspects of virtue as a whole.
In order to be temperate a man must be courageous:
in order to be able to resist the allurements of pleasure
he must be willing to endure the pain the resistance
involves. Similarly, in order to be courageous he must
be temperate,—at least in his desire for those kinds of
pleasure which he is called upon to forego in facing
danger, *e.g.*, the desire for life. Not less is the virtue of
social veracity implied in the virtue of devotion to truth
in thought and knowledge. The latter is, as has been
well said, merely an enlargement of the former. It is

the same virtue "exhibited, not in the mere normal interchange of ideas in language, but in the effort to represent things in thought as they really are in existence."

Similarly with the sub-species under the other-regarding virtue of benevolence. "Charity," we are told, "begins at home." In other words, duty to parent or child, friend or neighbour, is an essential side or aspect of duty to humanity. On the other hand, charity or love of humanity is the best guarantee against the exclusiveness which turns family affection into a vice. The same truth is illustrated by the saying, "Justice before generosity." Generosity, it is implied, presupposes justice. On the other hand, justice presupposes generosity, which is only justice adequately conceived.*

Finally, to take an extreme instance, it might be thought that the minor virtues of *amour propre* and politeness are clearly separable from those which refer to weightier matters of the law. But among the Greeks the virtue of magnanimity,† which corresponded in some degree to the first, was an essential quality in the best men, while the vice corresponding to the excess of it, viz.,

---

* It is, of course, the "adequate conception" which adds that splendour to the act which we indicate by calling it generous. The man who publishes the ruin of the company in which he holds most of the stock might be said to be generous to the public. He is only just, but he has an adequate conception of what justice implies. On the distinction between ideal justice, of which I am here speaking, and legal justice, see Bradley, *op. cit.* The former corresponds to equity as conceived by Aristotle: see *Rhetoric*, Book I., ch. xiii. (Welldon's Eng. Tr.); *Ethics*, Book V., ch. x.

† See Aristotle's famous description of the Magnanimous Man (*Ethics*, III.).

insolence (ὕβρις), was a noticeable element in the worst.
On the other hand, so close is the connection between
manners and morals that, just as politeness has been
defined as "benevolence in small things," so chivalry—
the cardinal virtue of the middle ages—might be defined
as "politeness in great ones."

With these explanations and exceptions, the following
table may be taken as a rough sketch of the exfoliation
of the good in some of its principal forms:—

§ 76. TABLE OF VIRTUES.

INTELLECTUAL VIRTUES.

MORAL VIRTUES.

Self-regarding (SELF-CONTROL).

Other-regarding.

Regarded, as by the Ancients, as the principle } = JUSTICE ["ordo amoris" (*St. Augustine*). "caritas sapiens" (*Leibnitz*).
of giving a citizen his due
Regarded, as by the Moderns, as the principle of seeking his good as } = BENEVOLENCE ["justice touched with emotion."
man

In voluntary relations.

Exercised in involuntary relations.

Humanity (PHILANTHROPY = caritas generis humani).

Church or Party (LOYALTY, ESPRIT DE CORPS).

Other People's. Toleration.

One's Own. Loyalty, etc.

In communication of it.

TEMPERANCE. SELF-RESPECT COURAGE. INDUSTRY. THRIFT.
(amour propre).

Neighbourhood (PUBLIC SPIRIT).

Country (PATRIOTISM).

Society POLITENESS ("benevolence in small things"), etc.

Family (FILIAL PIETY, etc.).

In business (HONOUR in discharge of debts, etc.).

In application of it to life.

SINCERITY. IMPARTIALITY. CONCENTRATION ACCURACY, etc. TRUTHFULNESS. CANDOUR. PROPER RESERVE. CONSIDERATION, etc.
(a form of courage).

In pursuit of truth.

In narrower sense, PRUDENCE; as when we say, A prudent housewife.

In broader sense, WISDOM as when we say, A wise counsellor

The relation between the moral and the intellectual virtues, *i.e.*, between devotion to duty on the one hand and devotion to truth and beauty on the other, suggests problems which the cursory treatment it has received in the text (pp. 180, 181) hardly can be said to solve. Thus it might be asked whether it is meant that the ground upon which devotion to art and science is deemed a virtue is the social usefulness of these pursuits. If this be so, it would appear from what has already been said of the relation between motive and morality (see pp. 59 foll.), that those only who in the studio or laboratory are consciously seeking the good of society or humanity are worthy artists or truthseekers. Whereas it is notoriously the case that the condition of the highest achievement in either field is that truth and beauty should be pursued for their own sakes, and not on account of any ulterior object. The difficulty is a real one, and may be shown to involve problems that lie outside the limits I have laid down for myself in the present treatise. Thus it would lead us to inquire, with regard to the ultimate relations of truth and beauty to one another, and of both to goodness, whether these three are really different from one another, as the above objection seems to presuppose, or whether they are not ultimately recognisable as different aspects of the one reality, the disinterested pursuit of them as different but co-ordinate forms of self-expression. Such an inquiry would obviously have been out of place in the text. Even here I can only give the conclusions to which I believe it would lead us—connecting them with the results of our previous examination into the nature of the good with a view to suggesting the solution of the above difficulty.

I have already defined the good as self-realisation. Morality means the human spirit taking flesh in the ordinary activities of daily life, so that, in realising, it may also be said to reveal itself. The condition of this self-revelation we have already seen to be its recognition of the objective relations of the moral order that we call society. We have now to add that the apprehension of the law of that objective order which we call the world of nature and of history, is as essential a condition of self-realisation on the side of intellect as the apprehension of moral law is on the side of the will. Hence it is that in the study of natural science, and still more obviously in the study of history and psychology, though we may appear to have gone outside of ourselves, we are, in reality, only investigating the contents of the human spirit itself (*cp.* p. 219 below). In the same way it may be shown that *art* is not concerned with a world that lies outside of ordinary human interests. Art does not, as common language would sometimes seem to imply, *create* a world of its own apart from ours: it *reveals* to us the world that lies within us and about us. Its function is not less interpretation than is that of science itself. It differs indeed from science in the medium which it chiefly employs. Its appeal is emotional rather than intellectual. Yet all true art, like true science, is ideal in that it serves to deepen our insight into the *meaning* of nature and of human life, and so to enlarge our knowledge of ourselves. If now, after these reflections, we return to the difficulty with which we started, we may note: (1) that it is a mistake to isolate truth and beauty from human good: they can only be admitted as rational ends in so far as they are elements in it. (2) While little is undoubtedly to be hoped for from the man who pursues science or art with a constant view to the economy of labour that ought to be practised in regard to what is merely a means to a further end, yet just as little is to be looked for from the man who in the pursuit of either of them forgets his relation to the larger world that embraces both. (3) The motive which constitutes an act good is never, as the preceding objection seems to imply, good in general, but is always some particular form of good. (4) Scientific and artistic activity under the conditions just mentioned being, as we have seen, such particular forms of good, are approved by mankind at large on the ground of the common interest which all have in the free play of thought and imagination, quite apart from any immediate public utility which may accrue from them.

On the difficulty here discussed, see Green, *op. cit.*, pp. 312 and 415; Alexander, *op. cit.*, pp. 123-6, 182-6, 257-9; Dewey, *op. cit.*, §§ xxxix. and lxxiii.; Lotze, *op. cit.*, p. 61. On the more general question of the relation of Intellectual to Moral virtue, see Aristotle, *Ethics*, Book VI.; and of Art to Morality, Plato, *Republic*, Book III., esp. § 401; Aristotle, *Poetics* (Cassell's National Library), pp. 23 and 39; Bosanquet, *Introduction to Hegel's Philosophy of Art*, esp. pp. 58, 105 foll.; *Essays in Philosophical Criticisms*, "The Philosophy of Art," by Professor W. P. Ker; Dewey, *Psychology*, pp. 195-201. For literary expression of the same truth, see, *e.g.*, Sir Philip Sidney's *Defence of Poesie* (Cassell's National Library); Spenser's Letter to Sir Walter Raleigh at beginning of the *Faërie Queene* (Globe Edition); Browning, *passim*, esp. Fra Lippo Lippi.

BOOK V

MORAL PROGRESS

CHAPTER I

§ 77. Differences of Standard which we may Neglect

WE have hitherto treated moral judgments as though they were universally applied in the same way, *i.e.*, as though there were only one good and one right, which is the same for all. The moral standard has been conceived of as something fixed and absolute, and even worked out into some detail in a system of virtues and duties representing the outline of a common ideal. Within this fixed standard indeed we have recognised differences. Thus it was pointed out that, inasmuch as the form under which each realises himself is prescribed for him by his station and its duties, this may be different for different classes and even for different individuals. The duty which the doctor at the bedside of a nervous patient recognises to verbal truthfulness is different from that of the witness in the box in a court of law. But this may be called a difference flowing from the very nature of the standard as a social one, rather than a difference in the standard itself. It is merely a difference of emphasis among duties which all recognise, and need not cause any further difficulty.

191

Nor is the absoluteness of the standard, as hitherto defined, affected by the kind of differences which, as distinguished from those just spoken of, we may call differences within the standard. They are the result of the co-existence of different standards in the same community. Thus the standard of morality in a circle of racing men or of horse-dealers will be different from that recognised by a Christian congregation. Even within the latter there will be differences, as between those who permit themselves to smuggle silk or tobacco at the Custom House or to take a ticket in a raffle-sale, and those who do not. Yet the difference is more apparent than real. It is the result of local depressions rather than of serious divergence of standard. In the case of the horse-dealer and the raffler, the higher standard is rather latent than non-existent, as is shown by the fact that it is possible to "convert" them. Differences of this kind, which have been called differences within the standard, cause no difficulty to ethics, and may be disregarded. In any time and country there is sufficient agreement as to the contents of the moral standard to lull suspicion in the unreflective as to more fundamental contradictions.

Another interesting form of variation is where different standards co-exist in the same individual. Thus, on being asked a question, a man will unblushingly reply with the query, "Do you ask me as a lawyer (doctor, stockbroker, etc.), or as a friend?" admitting thereby that he is the happy possessor of at least a pair of different standards, and intends to use the one or the other, according to circumstances. No more difficulty, however, need be caused by this case than by those already discussed. The man of many standards will probably admit, when closely pressed, that "a man's a man for a' that," and that there is a supreme standard which applies to him as sharing that distinction with his neighbours.

§ 78. Essential Differences in Standard involving Ethical Problem

It is the *comparative study of the moral codes of different times and countries* that first reveals the fact that the standard is relative in the sense that makes a difficulty for ethics, and causes practical alarm for the authority of the moral imperative. Not to go beyond historical times and the civilised nations of Europe, it is well known that, among the early Greek communities, the exposure of infants who were weak or deformed was not only deemed consistent with humanity, but advocated as necessary for the maintenance of the community and in the interests of morality. In the middle ages persecution for religious opinion differing from that of the majority was not only permitted, but approved of as a highly commendable form of religious zeal. At the present day, on the other side of the Channel, leading statesmen may meet in duel with the intent to maim or to kill without in any way losing caste or outraging the public conscience.

Nor is this variation in the standard in different times and countries confined to virtues which, like humanity and toleration, might be regarded as of secondary importance for the maintenance of society: it extends also to those which are usually regarded as primary, and as lying at the foundation of all social life. The children at Sparta were taught to steal: in the well-known story of

the child who stole a fox and permitted it to tear his
bosom rather than let it be discovered, the crime was,
not to steal, but to be found out. In the lives of the
saints among the Turks, as Locke informs us in his
celebrated chapter entitled "No Innate Practical Principles," the primary virtue of chastity had no place.

In respect to these and similar varieties of standard, it
is not, of course, enough to say that all respectable people
condemn these anomalies. The point is that they are
not anomalies, and that "all respectable people" in the
time and country in which they were practised approved
them. It would be a gross historical injustice to apply
our own standards in such cases. The virtue of the
Spartan boy must be judged by his own standard, not
by that of the shiny-faced urchin who creeps unwillingly
to school in an English village: so judged, it is heroic.
We have to recognise that in this sense goodness *is* a
different thing in different times and countries.

Is there then, it might be asked, no such thing as an
absolute standard of morality? Is morality not one, but
many and different? And are those justified who, upon
the basis of the latter hypothesis, draw the practical conclusion that, as opposed to what is "conventional" or
"expedient" for a community, there is no such thing
as "right"?

§ 79. The Unity of the Form of Virtue

The previous course of our argument has prepared us
for the answer to this question. At the very outset it
was shown that morality cannot consist in obedience to
a fixed code of rules. As opposed to this view, I
showed that morality is the conduct prescribed by an

end other than the momentary satisfaction of desire, which may indifferently be described as the satisfaction (*i.e.*, realisation) of the self as a whole (*i.e.*, the better self), or as the maintenance according to opportunity of the social system, which is only the other or objective side of this better self. This end is the principle of unity which underlies and "explains" the manifold imperatives in which the moral law expresses itself, inasmuch as it is the common root or stem of which, as the last chapter tried to show, they are exfoliations.

We have now only to apply these results to the question before us, in order to see that, underlying the apparent diversities in the contents of the moral standard, virtue is at all times one and the same. Wherever we have moral judgment approving a line of conduct as good, whether among the rudest band of savages or in those circles which in the most highly moralised countries in the world recognise the highest moral standard, it is seen to rest upon a more or less consciously recognised contrast between a permanent and a transient self: between the satisfaction of a higher, or true self, and of a lower, or apparent one.

Take, for instance, the savage who, when the enemy's hamlet has been taken by his tribe and the booty is in his power, instead of seizing the largest share he can and escaping to the solitary enjoyment of it in the woods, restrains his impulse in order to await his chief's own choice, and the subsequent distribution by the lot. What does this mean? It means that he restrains the instincts of his lower nature in view of a good, which in so far as he reflects upon it he recognises as his better self, viz., the social self which at this stage is represented by the rudely organised society of the nomadic tribe.

Or to revert to our previous illustration: the Spartan
boy is approved by the judgment of his time and
country because he sacrifices the pleasure-seeking, pain-
avoiding self, who would have done with the matter by
throwing away the fox; to an idea of a higher good, which
he represents to himself perhaps as "pluck" or "endurance," but which has value only in so far as it is
related to a moral order, loyalty to which the boy
recognises as part of his true self.

From these examples it will be seen that, while it is
undoubtedly true that morality differs from age to age
and under different circumstances, it springs in every
age and country from the same root; in other words,
while its matter or content varies its form or essence
remains the same.*

§ 80. The Relativity of the Standard as Condition of its Validity

But we may go further than this. For it further follows
from the argument in the previous chapters that the
relativity of the moral standard is not only compatible

---

* The above argument may be further illustrated from the
beginnings of morality in sub-human forms of life. (See Mr.
Spencer's article, *Nineteenth Century*, February 1890, since published in his book on *Justice*.) In these, as in the devotion of
the outpost elephant (*cp.* Professor Drummond's description of the
white ants in *Tropical Africa*) to the interest of the herd, we
have a shadow of human morality. Nature is *dreaming* of morality.
What makes the difference, of course, is the *power of conceiving* the
higher or common good. In saying so I do not intend to deny that
the lower animals may have the rudiments of such a conception
of a higher self. All I mean is, that it is the possession of such a
rudimentary conception, and not the mere empirical fact that the
lower animals exhibit such conduct, that justifies us in speaking
of sub-human justice, or any other sub-human virtue.

with the existence of a law which is absolute for each in
his special circumstances, but is a necessary condition
of the obligatoriness of morality and the validity of moral
judgment. We have already seen how this is so, within
certain limits, with respect to individuals living in the
same age and country. Duty with each of us was seen
to be relative to his station and circumstances. It is
this relativity which makes it duty for *me*. A law which
did not apply to me, in virtue of my place in the organism
of society, could not be binding upon me at all. It is
only an extension of the same principle to say that it is
because morality is always, and in all places, relative to
circumstances, that it is binding at any time and in any
place. The idea that it is otherwise comes from our
habit of conceiving of the moral law as isolated from the
social circumstances in which it rose, and as therefore
varying arbitrarily in different times and countries. The
error is corrected by recollecting that the variations we
are discussing are not accidental, but are organically
related to the circumstances of the time to which they
severally belong.

Thus, to go no further than our previous instances,
the practice of exposing infants (especially females*)
was justified at a time when it was necessary (or, which
comes to the same thing, was supposed to be necessary), in order to maintain that peculiar form of city-
state which flourished in Greece and Italy. When the
circumstances changed, when city-states had perished,
when higher ideas of the position of women began to
prevail, and when it became obvious that the outrage to

---

* See Merivale's *History of the Roman Empire*, Vol. V., pp. 56
and 303 *n.*

humanity that was involved in the practice was a greater
social evil than the burden thrown upon the community
by the necessity of maintaining an apparently useless
population, not only was exposure discountenanced, but
the public conscience was awakened to the duty of
making provision for their support.*

Similarly, intolerance dates from a time when, owing
to the intimate relations between State and Church (*e.g.*,
in the oaths of soldiers), it seemed to be of vital importance that no religious scruples of non-conformists (*e.g.*,
of the Christian soldiers in the Roman armies) should
interfere with the due performance of social obligations.
Intolerance ceased to be a virtue, and began to pass
over into the opposite category,† when, among other
changes, it began to be seen that freedom of thought
contributed more to the common good than any artificial
unity of religious belief.   As, then, the form of social
life varies from age to age in the course of natural evolution, morality, which, as we have seen (if it is to
be morality in the proper sense, and not mere blind
obedience to a traditional law), must represent "a quality
of the social tissue," must vary with it.

§ 81.   Further Difficulty

But perhaps this does not altogether meet the
difficulty.   Granted that there is a unity of form underlying the variations in the matter of moral obligation,

* See the Law of Constantine, quoted, Gibbon, II., p. 142
(Smith's edition).

† *Cp.* the definition of badness as a *survival*.   On the whole
subject of this chapter and book the student is recommended to
consult Book III. in the same work.

and, further, that the variations are a necessary in-cident in anything that can rightly be called a moral standard, a further question still remains.   If the social changes on which the variations spoken of depend are themselves only accidental circumstances dependent on efficient causes empirically discerned (and hitherto nothing has been said to show that they are not), morality comes, after all, to be nothing but that kind of conduct which supports one or other of the accidental changes in the phantasmagoria of social forms.   It is much, of course, to have established this underlying unity in varieties of standard, and to have proved that " the good " for the individual depends upon the good of the society of which he is a member.   But if these "goods" are only, after all, varieties of adaptation to environment blindly determined by natural causes, and are not united with one another in any order so as to suggest the idea of a universal or absolute good, there is, after all, no ground for the obligation to adopt the moral standard of any one of them rather than of another, except the accidental circumstance that our inherited aptitudes probably fit us for the conditions of life that obtain in that into which we have been born rather than those of any other.   And, if this be so, morality turns out, after all, to be relative in the sense for which the sceptic contends, viz., of resting upon no objective and universal moral order, but only upon one which is relative to the effects of accidental circumstances.*

The difficulty here suggested is a real one, involving as it does at least two distinct questions which press for an answer in the interest of the higher forms of practical

* For a clear statement of this difficulty, see Professor Knight's *Studies in Philosophy and Literature*, pp. 32 foll.

morality, perhaps of religion itself. They both, indeed, remind us of what was said in an earlier chapter of the impossibility of separating ethics from the study of the nature of the world as a whole, and man's relation to it. Nor, as we shall see, shall we be able altogether to escape without paying tribute to the spectre of metaphysics that has dogged our steps throughout. Meantime, however, it will be possible to avoid coming face to face with it, and to carry our explanation of the data of ethics a step further than we have hitherto done, by inquiring whether, amid the variety of forms the moral standard has been seen to take, any principle of unity is discernible in the light of which they may be seen to be more than isolated phenomena on a background of unintelligible change.

CHAPTER II

THE STANDARD AS PROGRESSIVE

§ 82. Clue to Solution of the Problem in Idea of Progress

THE question with which we ended the last chapter may be stated in a form which will make its connection with the results of our previous analysis plain to the student.

In seeking for an explanation of moral judgments, we traced them back to a principle of unity variously described as the end, standard, or ideal of conduct, in the light of which they were seen to be organically re-lated to one another and to the life of man as a social being. A new difficulty, however, rose when, on further investigation, we found that so far from there being one universally recognised standard, there exists a most bewildering variety in the standards or ideals that men have agreed to recognise. We were thus driven to ask whether this variety must be accepted as an ultimate fact, or whether all these different standards may not be susceptible of explanation in the same sense as the variety of the moral judgments under any one standard was found to be, by being shown to have their place as mutually related parts or elements in an organic whole. Is there, in a word, any larger conception of morality possible than that implied in the definition of it as a quality of the social tissue at any one time or place, in the light of which we may be enabled to establish a relation between conduct that supports any particular moral order, and some more universal end or purpose traceable in human history?

For the clue to the answer to the question, when so stated, we have not far to look. It is given in the conception of *progress* rendered familiar to us by evolutionist writers. Progress means change estimated in terms of approximation to an end,—the end being the principle of unity which harmonises and explains the successive steps. History, as contrasted with annals or chronicles, is the record, not simply of change, but of progress and *growth*. As applied to the life of nations and societies, evolution has made us familiar, not only with the idea, but also with the law of growth. Popularly stated, that law is that societies advance through successive stages of simultaneous differentiation and unification to ever higher and richer forms of life.

§ 83. Illustration of the General Law of Progress

This law hardly requires illustration. Mr. Spencer has formulated it in well-known terms to the effect that "an indefinite, incoherent homogeneity is transformed into a definite, coherent heterogeneity," profusely illustrating it in the fields of biology and social life. Thus the general course of biological evolution is seen to be from organisms such as the amœba, which are homogeneous and almost structureless, through fishes, reptiles, birds, to the highly differentiated structures of the mammals, and finally of man. A similar progress is traceable in the development of the social organism. At first this is simple and undifferentiated; all the members alike fish, and hunt, and fight. But with all its homogeneity, it is still a loose organisation, with little internal coherence. The functions are not specialised, the parts are comparatively independent of one another. With division of labour comes greater differentiation into castes and classes, and at the same time greater interdependence, greater unity and coherence, as these become mutually dependent on one another. As evolution proceeds the different forms of industry again differentiate into smaller groups or specialised industries. Similarly, the military forces are separated into departments, as of the home and foreign service, the army and the navy, etc.; the government into central and municipal, and each again into legislative, executive, and judicial.

§ 84. Progress of Humanity as a Whole

A process similar to that which takes place among individual nations may be seen to take place in the world at large, and in the human race as a whole. The growth here also is from a state of relative homogeneity and mutual isolation to greater heterogeneity, advancing *pari passu* with greater mutual interdependence and coherence among the parts. It is true that as yet this progress has been but fitful,* and that the indications of the growth of a universal human brother-

---

* As a whole, we have to recollect that "progress has many receding waves."

hood are but faint. If, however, we take the history of the nations of Europe and America during the last century, it cannot be doubted that some progress has been made. In so far as it is observable, it is in the direction indicated by our law. In the first place, we have a movement towards disruption and disintegration. This may be said to have begun in the great American War of Independence, and to have been continued in Europe in the national movement, which took its rise in the anti-Napoleonic reaction, created the German Empire, modern Greece, Italy, and Hungary, and cannot be said to have even yet spent itself. On the other hand, going on *pari passu* with this movement, we have the growth of international sympathy, industrial co-operation, and a community of intellectual interests, so that the Europe and America of to-day, in spite of the development of greater internal differences, are more united than ever before.*

If now we pass from these indications of the growth in the civilised world as a whole of a richer form of social and political organisation to the moral ideas and habits which, as we have seen, must at each stage be its support, we may expect to find a corresponding development, indicating at least a tendency towards a universal standard or ideal, which, as it unifies and gives significance to the separate varieties that have been developed in the progress, may be said to furnish the explanation of which we are in search.

* As illustrations of this progress may be mentioned International Arbitration, Labour Conferences, Industrial Exhibitions, the Postal Union, Laws of Copyright and of Extradition.

Confining ourselves to the history of particular nations, it is not difficult to show, not only that there is a definite progress in the moral standard, but that this progress obeys the law of all others as expounded above.

Thus, to take a well-known example, it is not difficult to show that, *pari passu* with the progress of the Jewish nation from a rabble of fugitive slaves to a great and highly civilised nation, there is a moral progress from the first elements of a standard in the Decalogue to the highly spiritualised morality of the later prophets and the Sermon on the Mount. A similar progress is traceable from the traditional and proverbial morality of early Greece to the reflective morality of the philosophers. The progress, moreover, is one from incoherent homogeneity to coherent heterogeneity. We have, on the one hand, a movement towards greater differentiation, as when the principles laid down in the ten commandments expand into the greater detail of the Sermon on the Mount (*e.g.*, the principle Thou shalt not kill being extended to minute particulars of daily life), or when the μηδὲν ἄγαν (nothing in excess) of traditional Greek morality differentiates into the elaborate table of the Aristotelian virtues.* On the other hand, we have a movement towards greater unity and coherence. To this corresponds in Jewish ethics the movement from the externality of the law to the "inwardness" of the Christian teaching. The law is "contained" in the golden rule (*i.e.*, is seen to be related to the spirit

* See *Ethics*, Books III. and IV.

or principle that underlies it as the particular to the universal), viz., love to God and to our neighbour. In the same way in Greek morality the integrating movement is plainly seen in the writings of the philosophers, who merely sum up the higher tendencies of their time when they exhibit the various forms of the good which constitute the common standard as flowing from a conscientious interpretation of the duties of a good *citizen.*

§ 86. Evolution of a Universal Moral Order

But this is not enough for our purpose. It is not enough to know that, in particular times or nations, the changes in the moral standard are determined by such a law of progress. We have to go further, and ask whether in morality as a whole throughout the history of humanity any such progress is discernible. The question is sufficiently wide. A complete answer to it could only be given in a general history of morality.* In writing such a history the historian would be met by a difficulty which is not felt in treating of the evolution of morality in a particular age or country, namely, that the process is not completed. It is comparatively easy to place the various stages in the development of Jewish and Hellenic morality in their true light, because it is possible to trace the leading features of the Jewish and Hellenic ideals as these fulfilled themselves in history. But where are we to find such fulfilment in a universal history? Here we must be satisfied with tendencies towards an ideal, into the nature of

* For a popular contribution to such a history, see Lecky's *History of European Morals.*

which we may have more or less insight, according to
the degree of our intellectual and moral culture, but
which at best is rather an object of faith than of sight.
Without committing myself to any speculative description of the general features of the moral ideal that is
working itself into shape as the common standard of
civilised humanity, I may try to illustrate the general
progress by considering one or two instances of it in the
particular virtues.

§ 87. Illustration from Courage *

Thus we may take the virtue of courage at two
successive stages in its development as part of the
common stock of moral ideas. It is the virtue which
the ancients delighted to honour, and of which Plato
and Aristotle have given careful and typical delinea-
tions.†   Among the Greeks it appears as the virtue
which is concerned with resistance to fear in the presence of danger and death. But when we compare the
Greek conception of it with our own, we become conscious of the same kind of difference which we saw above
characterised all higher as compared with lower forms
of organic life. It has become more differentiated.
As has been well pointed out,‡ our conception of the
kind of pains in reference to which the virtue is exhibited has greatly widened. Besides danger and death
in battle, there is the danger to health and life in the
mission field, the city slum, and the fever ward, which

---

* I take many hints in the ensuing illustrations from Green's
suggestive treatment of this subject, *Proleg. to Ethics*, Book III.

† See *Republic*, III., § 429, and *Nicomachean Ethics*, III., 6, 9.

‡ Green, *loc. cit.*, p. 279.

makes the foreign missionary, the slum sister, and the hospital nurse as heroic types among ourselves as the citizen soldier was among the Greeks. In these cases perhaps the difference is not so great but that we should class them all under the old title of courage, but, as the sphere of the virtue widens, parts of it tend to break away and appropriate to themselves new names. Thus, as the conception of the kind of pains in reference to which fortitude may be exhibited widens so as to embrace not only physical pains, but those which bear but a remote resemblance to them, not only those which may be inflicted by enemies, but those that spring from disagreement and misunderstandings with one's friends,* we have what is practically a new variety of the virtue —that which for want of a better name we call *moral* courage.

With this differentiation, which corresponds to the extension of the area covered by the virtue, there goes a greater integration, corresponding to the deepening of the consciousness of its significance. For it is just the relation which the virtue is felt to bear to human prog-ress in general which, while opening up new fields for its exercise, places the new forms thus generated, as well as the forms previously recognised, in closer relation to one another, and to virtue as a whole. A Greek would have been at a loss how to class the forms of virtue which we have mentioned above as typical of our own

---

* As examples of the pains in question may be taken those of the social ostracism inflicted by the majority of a particular class or profession upon an offending member, *e.g.*, by a church upon a clergyman who denounces its corruptions, or by the press upon an editor who denounces forms of social immorality that are generally winked at.

time.   He could hardly have denied that they were *like*
courage, but without the fully developed notion of
human brotherhood, he would have found it difficult
to invent a formula which could have given the clue to
the underlying identity.   We, on the other hand, while
recognising new forms of the virtue, perceive them only
to be extensions of it, required by wider conceptions of
that "society" in relation to which alone it has meaning.
At the same time, we interpret the virtue of courage itself
as only a particular form of virtue in general.   We recognise it as only "the form which individual and social
virtue take in presence of the obstacles, both moral and
physical, presented by the environment to the realisation
of the common human good." *

§ 88.   Illustration from Temperance

In further illustration of this truth we may quote the
virtue which the Greeks called Temperance, but which
we should call Self-control.   Along with extended ideas
of our duty to humanity, and especially to women, has
gone the application of the virtue to new relations.   An
obvious instance of the former is the appropriation of
the word "temperance" to a special form of self-control,
viewed as a duty to society at large as much as to
oneself or to the state.   From the general virtue of
self-control in matters of sense, self-control in matters
of drink has broken away, and set up, as it were, for
itself as an independent virtue.   Similarly, the range of
the virtue of self-control in matters of sex has immensely
widened.   Under the influence of new conceptions of

* I am indebted for this definition to *Lux Mundi*, p. 496
(1st ed.).

the position of women which were contained in germ in the Christian religion, a new emphasis came to be laid on the virtue in question, which, under the names of chastity and chivalry, is more than any other the key-stone of the modern form of social organisation.*

With this differentiation has gone hand in hand, as in the case of courage, a new conception of the relation of these forms to one another, and to virtue as a whole, corresponding to the movement of integration. Thus, to take our previous instance, it was difficult to see, so long as the view was confined to the narrow field of the Greek community, what was the precise relation of chastity to the other forms of temperance and to virtue as a whole. Accordingly, as is well known to any one familiar with Greek literature, it was the virtue most to seek in the character of the average good citizen. Even Socrates plays with unnameable forms of its corresponding vice, while Plato proposes a special exemption from its re-quirements as the reward of the youthful heroes in his "Republic." As a matter of fact, in the so-called mili-tary age, and in military circles in industrial ages, it has always tended to fall into the background.† It is only

---

* These examples, it may be noted by the way, are a further comment on Mr. Spencer's conception of an absolute ethics, and a state of society where all sense of duty, as involving pain, will dis-appear. As already pointed out, his theory is based on the notion that the environment is something definite and fixed. But, as we have just seen, our conception of the environment, and the obstacles it presents to the realisation of the good, changes with the deepen-ing of our conception of the nature of the good itself. Hence it involves as much pain (perhaps more, see above, p. 208 *n.*) to be courageous or chaste to-day as in Athens in the fourth century B.C. With progress "more is required of us."

† "It is not without reason that the earliest mythology united Ares

in view of a higher conception of the rights of women, as members of a universal fellowship and joint-partners in a common good, that the true significance of the virtue, and the relation of its various forms to one another and to the universal moral order, come into sight.

§ 89. Summary

Similar illustrations of the view for which I am contending might be drawn from the rise of the virtues of humility, mercy, truth, tolerance, class justice, esprit de corps,* etc., but sufficient has perhaps been said to show that the actual standard at any particular period, while undoubtedly relative to the special circumstances of the time and country, is not on that account an isolated and accidental phenomenon, but takes its place as a stage in the evolution of a universal moral order, from its relation to which in the last resort it derives its significance.† The practical conclusion to

and Aphrodite."—Aristotle, *Politics*, II., 9 (Bohn's Library, p. 62); see the whole passage.

* A simple example of the process of differentiation spoken of above is the Latin *pietas*, which is now represented by several virtues, chiefly those classed under involuntary social relations in our table (p. 186). Max Müller somewhere mentions a people (the Hawaiians) who have only one word (aloha) for love, friendship, gratitude, benevolence, and respect.

† The "universality" which is thus opposed to the "relativity" of the standard must not be misunderstood. After what has been already said, it cannot, of course, mean that morality can ever come to be "the same for all": duty is duty just because it is different for all. Nor can it mean the "finality" of any conceivable moral code. We have already seen sufficient reason to distrust the conception of a final or absolute ethics. It cannot even mean merely the "ubiquity" of the highest recognised standard, though

which the preceding discussion points is that moral
obligation at any particular stage rests, not merely on the
call to maintain a particular form of moral organisation,
but to maintain and forward the cause of moral order as
a whole.*

§ 90. Further Question

But before we can regard this conclusion as satisfactorily established, we have to encounter the second of the
two questions with which we were threatened at the end
of the last chapter.   Duty or obligation, as I have already
had occasion repeatedly to point out, rests on a personal
interest in a moral order, which when it is reflected upon
we recognise as "good," *i.e.*, as the revelation to man of
what he himself truly is or has it in him to become.
But how, it may be asked, can such an interest come to
attach to the moral order, the law of whose evolution we
have just been describing, if, as is commonly added, not
only the lines which it follows coincide with those of
biological evolution, but the cause which is at work in
producing it is in both cases the same?   If, as is
claimed, the process has been determined throughout by
the natural law of adaptation to environment and survival
of the fittest, and is thus explicable without reference to

this is undoubtedly an element in it.   The moral order which is
being evolved must be conceived of as universal, chiefly in the sense
that it represents the demands of the universal or rational element
in human nature.   My meaning will become apparent in the light
of considerations which I reserve for the next chapter.

* The endeavour to further evolution, especially that of the
human race, has been put forward by scientific writers as a "new
duty."   It would be better to say that it is a fundamental aspect of
old ones.

any free self-determination on the part of man, in what sense, it may be asked, can the result of the action of this biological law, viz., the existing moral order, be said to represent such a good? To answer this question, it is necessary that we should enter more fully than we have yet done into the question of the source or spring of the moral evolution I have been describing, in order to see whether it is true, as has just been suggested, that in accepting the evolutionist's statement of the course that moral evolution takes, we necessarily accept his account of the cause that explains it.

Simply stated, the question, then, is whether the enlargement and enrichment of the moral standard, which we have observed to be taking place, is sufficiently explained as the result of a mechanical process of adaptation to environment, determined, like biological evolution, at each step from without, and following the course laid down for it by purely natural causes; or whether there is not also required a reference to the action at each stage of a self-conscious intelligence, seeking its good as such, and evolving step by step from the raw material of its surroundings a system of social relations, in the maintenance and development of which that good may be found. The question, it will be acknowledged, is an important one at the stage of our argument at which we have arrived. For if the evolution is after all *merely* natural, the objections which we have ourselves urged against the scientific or evolutionary doctrine of the standard of morality will be found to apply after all, though at a later stage of the investigation and in a somewhat different form, to our own account. Unless the results of the progress can be shown to be elements in a more or less clearly conceived end or good, obligation, which we have seen to depend on the relation between conduct and personal good, is still without a foothold, even on the supposition of a universal moral order.

If we are to bring together the results just obtained with those of our previous argument, we cannot refuse to consider this difficulty.

CHAPTER III

THE STANDARD AS IDEAL

PART I

§ 91. The Question involves Metaphysical Considerations

THE difficulty started, but left unsolved, at the end of the last chapter, shortly stated, is: Whether progress in morality generally is explicable in terms of efficient causes as the result of adjustment to environment, as ordinarily interpreted; or whether it does not involve a reference to an end or ideal more or less consciously conceived by a subject, to whom changes in the environment and the adjustments rendered necessary by them are merely the opportunity for further self-realisation. So stated, the question introduces wide issues, which I cannot hope in the last chapter of a text-book like the present to treat as they deserve. Thus, to be satisfactorily answered, it would require to be discussed in close connection with the general question of the relation of the self or conscious subject as a whole to the world which constitutes its object or environment. This, however, would bring me into dangerous proximity with the metaphysical discussions which at the outset I abjured; so that I seem to be

caught in the dilemma of either abruptly ending my argument in the face of an unsolved difficulty, or using my
last chapter to break new ground and pass beyond the
limits I imposed upon myself. I shall not deceive
the reader, but confess to him my intention of choosing
· the latter alternative. The shock to him will, perhaps,
be mitigated by the recollection that in the last two or
three sections we have admittedly been prospecting on
the borders of that thorny region. In the following
section I shall ask him boldly to step across with
\e and take a look at things at home from the other
side, at the same time promising not to lead him further
into its dangerous wildernesses than is necessary in order
to get a clearer view of the point we have reached and
the path by which we have come.

§ 92. Consciousness as Active Principle in Knowledge

The old-fashioned view of the relation of the conscious
subject to the external world is that the knowledge of the
latter is impressed upon it from without. The subject
is the passive receptacle of feelings, sensations, and ideas
which *come* to it. Progress consists in the storage, classification, and acquired power of recalling and utilising these
possessions at the proper moment. A little reflection,
however, is sufficient to dispel the illusion on which this
view is based. Thus, to take the lowest element in
knowledge, sensation, it is a commonplace of the text-
books to point out that in the last analysis the so-called
external world reduces itself to stimuli imparted to the
physical organism. To a certain extent it may be said
that differences in sensation depend on differences in the
stimuli, which in turn resolve themselves into differences

in the rate of velocity in the vibrations which cause them. Vibrations of a low rate of velocity affect us through the sense of touch, as a feeling of jar. When the velocity reaches some 20,000 per second we have a sensation of sound. Above 40,000 per second we no longer hear them. When they reach a much higher number we begin to have sensations of colour, beginning with red, and passing through the chromatic scale to violet. Above a certain point they are too numerous to be responded to by the visual apparatus, and light disappears. In all which the point to be observed is that, as it has been well put, "out of what is in itself an undistinguishable, swarming continuum, devoid of distinction or emphasis, *our senses make for us* . . . a world full of contrasts, of sharp accents, of abrupt changes, of picturesque light and shade." So that even on the plane of the senses which we share with the lower animals, the world of knowledge is not so much a revelation of an external universe as a revelation of our own nature as sentient beings.

Coming to the subject or self, as a conscious principle of unity amid the variety of presentations, we may see that this is even more obviously true. It is not, of course, contended that the mind can evolve knowledge from its inner consciousness, any more than sensations can call themselves into being without aid from external stimuli. What is asserted is, that it does not approach the world as a passive receptacle, or, according to the well-known metaphor, a *tabula rasa*, on which the world to be known imprints itself. From the outset it is an active principle of interpretation, to which the world comes as a system of signs, like the signals received by the clerk at a telegraphic depôt, rather than as a reflection in a mirror, or the impression imprinted by the seal upon the

wax. Moreover, the standard of interpretation is furnished by itself; and the world which it builds up out of
the material supplied it from without is a memorial to
the fundamental principles it brings with it to the work
(*i.e.*, to the chief features of its own inner nature), rather
than to any world that exists independently of it.

§ 93. The Unity of the World as Postulate of Thought

The detailed account of these principles is the subject-
matter of philosophy as the theory of knowledge and
reality. It is sufficient for our purpose to point out
that the primary feature which distinguishes a conscious self from a merely sentient subject is that it
asserts its "personal identity" as the underlying unity
of its transient experiences. Even in its most elementary stage, the world of such a self is a unity in a
sense which it is not (apparently) to the lower animals.
Hence the fundamental principle it brings with it to
the interpretation of the signs supplied it from without * is that they should form an intelligible unity or
whole. This is the ideal to which, even at its most
elementary stage, it demands that knowledge shall correspond. If it has no other unity to the mind of the
savage or the child, the world at least possesses the
unity of being in one space, its events in one order of
succession in time. But this order is not something
given. It is the mind's first effort to embody its ideal in
the data of experience. Advance, moreover, does not

---

* I use the popular language in permitting myself to speak of
signs, material, etc., coming from *without*. Metaphysics, of course,
has something further to say on this externality.

come from without by the mere heaping up of experiences.   It is an advance to higher forms of unity among them, and this advance is forced upon the subject by the demand which its own nature, as active intelligence, makes upon it,—the demand, namely, to see in the so-called external world an ever more perfect embodiment of the ideal of unity which itself supplies.   From this point of view, therefore, progress in knowledge has to be looked at rather as a progressive revelation to the self of its own nature than as the unfolding of an external world to an observing subject.*

From all this two results follow.   (1) The sciences, as they exist at any time, are not to be looked at as the mere accumulation of generalisations from experience and the deductions which are drawn from them, but as actual embodiments of mind.   They are the best up-to-date account which mind can give of itself—the reflection or mirror of its inner nature so far as revealed upon this globe.   (2) Progress comes from within.   New objects and events are the *occasion*, not the *cause* or primary

* "Nervous signs," says Bowne (quoted, James's *Principles of Psychology*, I., p. 220), "are the raw material of all knowledge of the outer world. . . . But, in order to pass beyond these signs into a knowledge of the outer world, we must posit an interpreter who shall read back these signs into their objective meaning.   But that interpreter, again, must implicitly contain the meaning of the universe within itself, and these signs are really but excitations which cause the soul to unfold what is within itself.   Inasmuch as by common consent the soul communicates with the outer world only through these signs, and never comes nearer to the object than such signs can bring it, it follows that the principles of interpretation must be in the mind itself, and that the resulting construction is primarily only an expression of the mind's own nature.   *All reaction is of this sort; it expresses the nature of the reacting agent.*"   Cp. Note at end of preceding book.

source, of intellectual development. What Aristotle says of political revolutions is true of scientific progress: it is the outcome of great causes and small occasions. The fall of an apple may be the *occasion* of the discovery of a law which may be said to have remade the world for scientific men; but the *cause* is in the ideal of a self-consistent system of planetary movements, as that was conceived in Newton's mind. So generally, unless consciousness were the seat of an ideal of a completely unified world of mutually related parts, progress, in any intelligible sense, would be impossible. It is only in so far as the new materials are interpreted in the light of its own principles, and are seen by the mind further to fill out and illustrate the ideal it cherishes of completed knowledge or of a completely knowing self, that there can be said to be growth and progress in knowledge.*

§ 94. Conscience and Consciousness

Now conscience is only another side of consciousness. It is in the field of practice what consciousness is in the field of knowledge. This fundamental identity is already indicated in the words themselves. Consciousness (*conscire*) is the sense we have of ourselves, as realised in the mode of activity we call knowledge; conscience (also *conscire; cp.* Old Eng. *inwit*) is the sense we have of ourselves as realised in conduct. Hence we may expect to

---

* Practically this dependence of the mind in intellectual progress upon its ability to see in the new facts a further revelation of itself takes the form of the familiar statement that intellectual effort depends upon *interest*,—interest being the emotional satisfaction which an object gives us as a possible means of further self-realisation. *Cp.* Dewey, *op. cit.*, §§ xxxiv. foll.; also on general subject of this section, § xl.

find interesting analogies cropping up between them in respect to the relations discussed in the last paragraph. Of these it is here important to note (1) that the objective world of human relations is to conscience what the external world of experience is to consciousness. Just as we saw that, apart from the interpreting and constructive power of the human mind, the external world is merely a chaos of nervous movements, so, apart from the interpreting power of conscience, the relations and institutions of society are mere physical facts without moral meaning.* (2) As the principle of interpretation in the former case is the ideal which the conscious self cherishes of a unified world of experience, representing its own complete realisation as a principle of knowledge, so the principle which conscience brings to the interpretation of external circumstances is the ideal of a system of moral relations, representing its own realisation as a principle of conduct. (3) As, finally, progress in knowledge was shown not to come from without, but to be the result of the inner demand of the self for a more and more perfect embodiment of its ideal of unified knowledge, so progress in morality has its spring, not in mere

---

* The question is sometimes asked whether any sane person is wholly devoid of conscience. I am not here concerned to find the answer to this conundrum, but merely to point out that in proportion as any one approaches such a limit, moral relations and institutions tend to lose their meaning for him. To Hedda Gabler, in Ibsen's play of that name, moral sacrifices are simply unintelligible. She does not understand those who make them. Her dislike of them (*e.g.*, of her aunt) is merely the dislike of a clever girl to what is stupid and unreasonable. If she had had a little more conscience, her dislike would have turned into hatred. For in that case she would have recognised them as persons whose conduct was a standing reproof to her own almost fiendish selfishness.

adjustment of the self to changing circumstances, but in the interpreting, constructive power of conscience finding in new circumstances the occasion for the further realisation of its ideal of rationalised and unified conduct.

§ 95. Relation of Conscience to Social Environment

If now we return from this somewhat abstract discussion, and ask what is its bearing on the question with which we started, viz., the relation of the subjective element in morality (*i.e.*, conscience) to the objective (*i.e.*, social conventions and institutions), we have to note :—

(1) That the above argument has confirmed from a new point of view the doctrine developed in a previous chapter, viz., that the system of social institutions, among which the individual finds himself, is only the other or objective side of the organic system of impulses and desires that constitute his inward nature.   It is so because, as we have just seen, it is the result of the reaction upon his environment of a self-conscious, or, as we may now say, "conscientious" being, who seeks to create out of it a system of relations corresponding to the ideal which his nature, as conscious intelligence, forces upon his notice.   It thus comes to the individual as a species of objectified conscience.   It supplies him with an objective expression of the chief contents of the ideal which he himself, as sharing the intelligence and conscience embodied in these forms, is called upon to make actual.   Practically, this is of immense value to him.   For, in the first place, he is not left to the subjective witness of his own reason to interpret the demands of conscience.   These are already writ large in the social relations into which he is born, or, as we previously

expressed it, in his station and its duties. Secondly, these relations present him with a standard by which he may correct his own subjective judgments. Conscience, if left to itself, is liable to run into all kinds of caprice. Unless its judgments are constantly checked by a reference to actual social requirements, as by a kind of "double entry," it may easily be transformed from a guarantee of social solidarity into a principle of isolation and anarchy.*

(2) But, while the social environment is thus an invaluable aid to the individual conscience in interpreting its own ideal, the conscience is always reacting on the environment. A man's "station and its duties" is not the fixed quantity we are apt to suppose. It is not a "bed of Procrustes" to which he has permanently to adapt himself; rather it is a "leaden rule" which has to adapt itself to him. The good life is not, except in a society of Podsnaps, a treadmill of recurring duties, keeping a man in a state of stable equilibrium with his environment. It is a "moving equilibrium," changing and expanding as new circumstances arise, which conscience interprets in its own way as "further calls." † New interests develop from the old ones, which, conscientiously pursued, tend to change the whole aspect of his environment.‡ While, therefore, it is true that a man's duties at any particular moment may be expressed in terms of

---

* It has been observed that Intuitionalist thinkers, who in their ethical analysis begin and end with conscience, tend to be individualists in politics.

† As Lowell has it—

> "New occasions teach new duties;
> Time makes ancient good uncouth."

‡ A familiar instance is when a man marries.

definite social relations, yet, as a being with a conscience
(*i.e.*, a moral ideal), he can never find adequate expression
for himself in them, but has to seek new occasions for
the exercise of his virtue or excellence as a man.   He
has "ideas beyond his station." Progress for himself
and the society in which he lives depends upon his following their lead into new social combinations, resulting in
a richer form of life for himself and others.*

§ 96. Is the Ideal Social or Personal?

A question might here be raised as to whether the
ideal which is thus seen to be the source of progress
is primarily one of a better form of social life or a

---

* These two aspects of the moral life have found so admirable
a literary expression in Mazzini's essay "On the Condition of
Europe" (see *Essays*, Camelot Series, p. 286) that I cannot
refrain from quoting him :—"Life is one: the individual and
society are its two necessary manifestations; life considered singly
and life in relation to others. . . . The individual and society are
sacred; not only because they are two great *facts* which cannot be
abolished, and which consequently we must endeavour to con-
ciliate, but because they represent the only two *criteria* which we
possess for realising our object, the truth,—namely, *conscience* and
tradition. The manifestation of truth being progressive, these two
instruments for its discovery ought to be continually transformed
and perfected; but we cannot suppress them without condemning
ourselves to eternal darkness. We cannot suppress or subalternise
one without irreparably mutilating our power. Individuality, that
is to say, conscience, applied alone, leads to anarchy; society, that is
to say, tradition, if it be not constantly interpreted and impelled
upon the route of the future by the intuition of conscience, begets
despotism and immobility. Truth is found at their point of inter-
section. It is forbidden, then, to the individual to emancipate
himself from the social object which constitutes his task here
below, and forbidden to society to crush or tyrannise over the
individual."

higher type of personal character.* Different answers
will probably be given in the case of different individuals.   Where sympathy and imagination are active,
the inner call tends at once to be translated into terms
of higher forms of social well-being.   On the other
hand, where sympathy and imagination are sluggish,
but the will strong and the purpose earnest, the call may
come rather in the form of a demand for greater purity
of motive and more consistent character.   Each of these
forms of conscientiousness has its advantages and its
dangers. The advantage of the former is the enthusiasm
that goes along with it.   Effort is inspired and sustained
by the vision of the new heavens and the new earth.
The danger is that the cultivation of qualities of character, on which, in the last resort, all social well-being
depends, should be neglected for the sake of "quick
returns" in the shape of increase of general happiness.
The advantage of the latter is that the will is bent on
being itself that which, in so far as general well-being is
the end, it must wish all other wills to be.   The corresponding danger is that the essentially social character
of all forms of goodness should drop out of sight, and
that wholeness (in the sense explained in Book IV.)
should be sacrificed to holiness.   The two attitudes, however, can never be entirely separate in any one whom
we judge morally good.   Purity of will is only possible
to one who is absorbed in the higher interests of life.
On the other hand, unless we are to suppose it possible

---

* For the points of contrast and the fundamental identity in the
saintly and the reforming type of character, see Green's *Prolegomena*,
Book IV., ch. v.; and on the subject of conscientiousness generally,
ibid., pp. 323-37; Martineau, *op. cit.*, Vol. II., pp. 59 foll.; Alexander, *op. cit.*, pp. 156-60; Dewey, *op. cit.*, § lxiii.

to gather "grapes of thorns, or figs of thistles," social progress cannot be safe in the hands of those in whom the desire for social improvement does not involve a keen sense of personal responsibility, and a high ideal of the kind of life required in those who claim to be its prophets and evangelists.

Part II

§ 97. Evolutionary Account of Moral Progress

The reader will have already perceived that the answer to the question with which we closed the last chapter is involved in the foregoing argument. It remains for me only further to illustrate what has just been said by indicating how the ordinary account of the evolution of morality requires to be supplemented, in order to bring it into harmony with the view I have taken throughout of the nature of moral judgment and the ground of obligation. In doing so I shall assume that the evolutionists' treatment of the origin and growth of morality is fairly familiar to the reader, and that a short allusion to it will suffice.

In this treatment attention is called to the important part which the struggle for existence and the law of natural selection have played in the evolution of morality. Thus, it is shown how at the outset the pressure of environment forced the members of hostile tribes into closer union with one another, developing social solidarity, and with it the virtues on which it depended. Progress was conditional on the survival of those tribes whose members best responded to the social requirements thus forced upon them, and on the consolidation and propagation of the form of social organisation and the standard of morality corresponding to this response. In this way, to take familiar examples, the Judaic organisation asserted itself triumphantly against the Canaanitic; the Greek maintained itself against the Persian, and ultimately, in the conquests of Alexander, overcame its ancestral rival in the East; the Roman superseded the Greek. In modern times, the Protestant has, on the whole, been victorious over the Catholic; the democratic and industrial over the feudal and military.

In the common account of the mode in which the law of natural selection acts in the sphere of morality, the emphasis has usually been laid on the analogy between social and biological evolution. Little attempt has been made to note the characteristic differences in the two cases. Recently the subject has received more careful treatment from evolutionary writers,* by whom it is pointed out that, whereas in the case of the lower animals and of man in the earlier stages of his development survival of the fittest is purchased at the price of the destruction of the unfit, in the later stages of social evolution this is less and less the case. Thus, to illustrate from our previous examples, the conquest of Canaan by the Jews does not appear, in spite of the reiterated instructions of priests and prophets, to have been followed by the extirpation of the inhabitants of the land. Nor were the conquests of the Greeks and Romans followed, as a rule, by the annihilation of their enemies. The reason of this difference is that with the growth of humanitarian feeling the conflict came to be one between social and moral ideals, rather than between

---

* *E.g.*, Mr. Alexander, whose application of the law of natural selection to the progress of the moral ideal is worthy of study, *op. cit.*, pp. 353 foll.

nations as physical aggregates. The aim of the con-
queror is not to exterminate, but to "convert" the
conquered by imposing his ideal upon him. As a rule,
he succeeds, as when Greek culture and modes of thought
overspread the East in the track of the armies of
Alexander; or when (to take a modern instance) the
expeditions of the Revolution armies under Napoleon
carried the ideas of the French Republic through the
length and breadth of Europe.* In other cases the ideal
of the conquered coalesced with or even overcame that
of the conquerors, as was notably the case on the conquest of Greece and Judæa by Rome, and of Rome
itself by the Goths.†

The conflict of ideals within a particular society serves
still better to illustrate this distinction. If swords have
not yet been beaten into ploughshares and spears into
pruning hooks, they have at any rate on the field of party
warfare been exchanged for the pen, the platform, and
the garden party. The end is victory as before, but the
means are persuasion and education (which, as has been
well said, is only an organised method of persuasion).
So far from exterminating, or even injuring, its political
opponent, a victorious party heaps coals of fire upon his
head by educating his children in the victorious and
presumably the better ideas.

---

* Substituting. *e.g.*, in Germany, the Code Napoleon for the feudal
system of land tenure that had previously existed. At the present
moment we have in Alsace-Lorraine an interesting conflict proceeding
between the French and German ideals of life and organisation.
As Mr. Gladstone once pointed out, the justification of the retention
of these provinces by Germany will be its power of morally assimi-
lating them with itself, *i.e.*, of imposing its ideal upon them.

† In which cases *Victi victoribus leges dederunt.*

To complete this sketch of the evolutionists' account of the actions of "natural law in the spiritual world," it remains to be pointed out how, in the view of certain economic writers, all the great steps in moral progress are connected with changes which the necessity of adaptation to material environment has brought about. Thus, the spread of humanitarian feeling and ideas in the early Roman empire is claimed as the result of the changes which followed upon the break-up of the older agricultural basis of society in Italy and throughout the world, the development of vast industries directed by Roman princes, and the universal system of trade and finance introduced by Roman capitalists. Again, it is pointed out that the release of the serfs in the middle ages, which by some is claimed as a step in moral progress, only followed the break-up of the social system which had rendered it necessary for the baron to support crowds of small owners or crofters upon the soil. Slave-emancipation, in more recent times, was, in like manner, the result of the discovery that the system of industry founded upon slavery was an unprofitable one, and unable to compete with free labour. Lastly, not to multiply examples, the French Revolution and all the moral enthusiasm it awakened had their roots in the break-down of an effete system of national finance, as is well known to all readers of the Second Book of Carlyle's History of that event.

§ 98. How this Account requires to be Supplemented

Now if these facts are put forward as representing the external or material aspect of moral progress, their importance can hardly be exaggerated. The study of them bears much the same relation to ethics as physiology does to psychology. As the study of the nervous system and of the brain throws important light on the origin and evolution of mind, so the study of the external conditions of moral progress may be expected to throw important light on the origin and contents of morality. If, however, they are put forward as a complete account of the origin and growth of *moral ideas*, we shall find reason in the preceding argument for being on our guard. As *ideas* these are in the mind, as *moral* ideas in the conscience, of individual men, and in neither case can they be simply consequences of material changes. So far from external changes being the cause of them, these changes are only operative as occasions of progress in so far as they are interpreted by the reason and conscience of individuals in the way explained above.

Thus, the struggle for existence has undoubtedly tended to promote the survival of tribes whose solid and coherent organisation rendered them the fittest, and accordingly may be said to be one of the conditions of the evolution of those virtues which, like loyalty to king or chief, went to support this organisation. But this is only one side, the *out*side of the truth. Before the solidarity—the *loyalty;* and before the loyalty, or constituting the loyalty —an *idea* in the mind of the individual member of an end or form of self to be realised in the loyal conduct. It is not, of course, maintained that, at the early stage of evolution referred to, we are to look for a fully developed conscience any more than for a fully developed reason. All that is asserted is that, so far as there is consciousness at all (*i.e.*, so far as we can say that we are dealing with *human* history), there is involved in its presence more than a mere instinctive response to the external circumstances requiring adjustment to environment. This something more is, in the case of the loyal member of the community, an interpretation of the circumstances as an occasion to realise an end which belongs to him as man. Whether this end is conceived of in terms of internal worth—in which case the circumstances would be interpreted as an occasion for exhibiting the qualities and developing the character of a man—or of social good—in which case the conduct would seem to be demanded by the

> " Relations dear, and all the charities
>   Of father, son, and brother "—

it does not matter. The point is that the *conception* is there as an ideal, and, as such, is the vital element in the stage of progress represented by our illustration.

Similarly in the other examples which were cited above. The Jews were no doubt forced into closer union under their theocratic government by the pressure of their environment, and the necessity to present a solid resistance to their enemies. But to interpret this necessity in terms to which the human spirit could respond, to formulate the duties which were involved in the maintenance of their peculiar form of organisation as elements in a national life, and incorporate them in such a body of moral and religious precept as we find in their literature, required the interpreting, *idealising* reason of successive generations of law-givers, judges, and priests. Again, humanitarian ideas began to spread after Roman conquest had broken down the proud isolation of Jew and Greek; but before the new conditions introduced by the *Pax Romana* could become the occasion of a moral advance, they required the moral enthusiasm of the

Christian apostles * and the reflective insight of the Stoic
philosophers to interpret them. The Protestant form
of organisation is likely to survive the Roman Catholic,
owing to its superior adaptation to the environment; but
part of that environment is just the demand of the human
spirit for liberty of thought and conscience as an essential
element in the ideal of personal good. The democratic
form of government is undoubtedly that which is best
adapted to modern conditions, and may be expected to
survive and propagate itself; but it was the moral enthusiasm for the "rights of man" at the end of the last century
and the beginning of this, and not the break-down of an
economic system, which created modern democracy.†
With regard to slavery we have already seen how the
moral consciousness of mankind protested against it, as
early as the time of the Cynics (p. 117). It is true,
indeed, that it was economically played out as a form
of labour before its abolition came, and that, apart from
the apprehension of this fact, its general abolition among
civilised nations might have been delayed for several
generations. Yet it may well be doubted whether, even
after the discovery of its economic failure had been
made, this would in itself have been sufficient to break
through the crust of prejudice and habit, behind

* *Cp.* George Eliot's fine saying, "The great world-struggle of
developing thought is continually foreshadowed in the struggle of
the affections *seeking a justification for love and hope.*"

† Napoleon has been called "the matricide of democracy," in that,
while it was the democratic movement in Europe which may be said
to have given him birth, he did his best to strangle it. The saying
might be true if democracy were the effect merely of adaptation to
environment, and not an elemental force in human nature, whose
expression in suitable social forms an individual may delay, but
cannot prevent.

which the institution was entrenched, but for the moral
enthusiasm which accompanied, and, on any rational
interpretation of history, was independent of it.

Wherever then, as in all these cases, we have accompanying changes in the material conditions of human
existence, an extension and enrichment of the moral
standard in the sense explained in the preceding chapter, this is to be traced, in the last resort, to the reaction
upon the changed circumstances of conscious intelligence
applying, in the method characteristic of it as such, a
higher standard than is as yet represented by any existing form of social organisation.

§ 99. The Social Reformer and Martyr

The interpreter and administrator of this ideal
standard is the social reformer, with his brother, the
martyr for ideal causes. As the power to explain the
phenomena of their lives—their manifest disregard of all
standards of individual or social utility in the narrower
sense—may be taken as the criterion of any ethical
theory, I may close this discussion by submitting the
view set forth in the preceding pages to this test.
That the "naturalistic" theory of ethics has failed to
satisfy it, we may take upon the authority of the admissions of the most candid of its exponents.* On the
view we have developed, on the other hand, these phenomena are perfectly comprehensible. The reformer I
should define merely as one who sits closer to conscience
in the sense explained than the run of his neighbours.
He is the child of the ideal, as opposed to the majority

* See Mr. Leslie Stephen, *Science of Ethics*, pp. 428, 430.

around him, who might be described as "the children of
the *status quo*," * and is accordingly as "one born out of
due season." But this does not mean that existing forms
are meaningless to him. On the contrary, he is just
the man who understands them, for he can see them as
organically related to the ideal which he cherishes, bearing the same relation to primitive conceptions of that
ideal as the institutions or reforms he works for bear to
its fuller development in his own mind and that of his
party or disciples. Loyalty, however, to ancestral wisdom does not with him consist in blind acceptance of its
creations. On the contrary, such blind acquiescence in
the *status quo* is treason to the idealising, innovating spirit
to which, in its own day, the *status* itself was due. As
has been well remarked, the opponents of useful reforms
are drawn from the same class as at the outset blindly
resisted the establishment of the form or institution to
which they themselves blindly cling. Those who build
the sepulchres of the prophets and garnish the tombs of
the righteous are the children of those who slew them.
On the other hand, in demanding the reform of institutions as they are, the reformer is only demanding room
for a fuller expression of the ideal which they represent,
and apart from which they are meaningless. He is only
carrying on the work which the reason and conscience
of those who went before have begun, reacting on the
given conditions as his own reason and conscience now
react. He feels himself the representative of those
who have gone before. Their ideal is his ideal. It
constitutes his true self. His deepest interest is to
realise it. Talents, time, fortune, friends, station, life

* M. Arnold's libellous definition of the English aristocracy.

itself, are of value to him only in so far as they offer him an opportunity of working for it.   Apart from such opportunity, they are valueless to him; if they rob him of it (as they will if, in order to retain them, he is tempted to deny the supremacy of his ideal), they may even become an object of hatred and disgust.   To love his life in this sense may be to lose it; to hate it may be to find it.

THE END

BIBLIOGRAPHY

Of some of the Chief English Works on Ethics (arranged as much as possible according to Schools and Dates).

I. EARLY INTUITIONALISM

Shaftesbury, (3rd) *Earl* (1713) ; ed. Hatch, with notes. 1869.
Butler, Bishop Joseph. *Sermons* (1726) ; *Dissertation on Virtue* (1729). (Both in Butler's *Analogy and Sermons*. Bohn's Library.)
Hutcheson, Francis. *System of Moral Philosophy* (1755). See T. Fowler's *Shaftesbury and Hutcheson*. 1883.
Smith,* Adam. *Theory of the Moral Sentiments* (1759).

II. LATER INTUITIONALISM

Price, Richard. *Review of Chief Questions and Difficulties of Morals* (1757).
Reid, Thomas. *Outlines of Moral Philosophy* (1793) ; ed. McCosh. 1863.
Stewart, Dugald. *Outlines of Moral Philosophy* (1793); ed. McCosh. 1869.
Whewell, William. *Elements of Morality* (1848). 1864.
Calderwood, Henry. *Handbook of Moral Philosophy* (1872). 1888.

* There are other elements in Adam Smith's ethics which relate him to the Utilitarians. The same is true, though in lesser degree, of all the earlier writers here mentioned.

Martineau, James. *Types of Ethical Theory*, 2 vols. (1885).
1886.
Lawric. S. S. *Ethica.* 1885.
Porter, Noah. *The Elements of Moral Science.* 1885.

III. EGOISTIC HEDONISM

Hobbes, Thos. *Elementa Philosophiæ de Cive* (1642). *De Corpore Politico; or, the Elements of Law, Moral and Political* (1650). *Leviathan* (1651). 1885.
Mandeville, Bernard de. *The Fable of the Bees* (1714).

IV. UTILITARIANISM

Locke.* John. *Essay concerning the Human Understanding,* Book I., chs. iii. and iv. (1690). 1868.
Hartley, David. *Observations on Man* (1748).
Hume, David. *Enquiry concerning the Principles of Morals* (1751). *Works:* ed. Green and Grove. 4 vols. 1882. *Essays, Literary, Moral, and Political* (1742). 1875.
Paley, William. *Principles of Moral and Political Philosophy* (1785). 1859.
Bentham, Jeremy. *Introduction to the Principles of Morals and Legislation* (1789). 1876. Edited in 2 vols. separate from *Deontology* (posthumous). *Works* by J. Bowring (1834).
Mill, James. *Analysis of the Human Mind,* chs. xvii.-xxiii. (1829). 1878.
Mill, John Stuart. *Utilitarianism* (1863). 1871.
Bain, Alexander. *Mental and Moral Science* (1868). 1872.
Sidgwick, Henry. *Methods of Ethics* (1874). 1890.
Hodgson, Shadworth H. *Theory of Practice,* 2 vols. 1870.
Fowler, Thomas. *Progressive Morality.* 1884.
v. Gizycki, G. *Students' Manual of Ethical Philosophy;* adapted by Stanton Coit. 1889.

* Locke is difficult to class. See Sidgwick's *History of Ethics;* Fowler's *Locke* (*English Men of Letters*), ch. ix. init.

V. Evolutionary Ethics

Darwin, Charles. *Descent of Man* (1871), chs. i.-v. and xxi. 1883.
Spencer, Herbert. *Data of Ethics* (1879). 1887.
Clifford, W. K. *Lectures and Essays* (1879). 1886.
Stephen, Leslie. *Science of Ethics*. 1882.
Alexander, Samuel. *Moral Order and Progress*. 1889.

VI. Early Idealists

Cudworth, Ralph. *Eternal and Immutable Morality* (posth. 1688).
Cumberland, Richard. *De Legibus Naturæ* (1672).
Clarke, Samuel. *Boyle Lectures* (1704).

VII. Nineteenth-Century Idealists

Caird, Edward. *The Critical Philosophy of Kant* (1877), 2 vols. 1890.
Green, T. H. *Prolegomena to Ethics* (1883). 1887.
Bradley, F. H. *Ethical Studies*. 1876.
Sorley, W. R. *Ethics of Naturalism*. 1885.
Courtney, W. L. *Constructive Ethics*. 1886.
Royce, Josiah. *Religious Aspect of Philosophy*. 1887.
Mackenzie, J. S. *Introduction to Social Philosophy*. 1890.
Lotze. *Practical Philosophy*. 1890.
Dewey, J. *Outlines of a Critical Theory of Ethics*. 1891.

History

Sidgwick, H. *Outlines of the History of Ethics* (1886). 1888.
See also Sonnenschein's *Library of Philosophy* (in progress).

UNIVERSITY MANUALS

A NEW SERIES OF
USEFUL AND IMPORTANT BOOKS

EDITED BY PROFESSOR WM. KNIGHT

CHARLES SCRIBNER'S SONS, Publishers

THIS Series, published by John Murray in England
and Charles Scribner's Sons in America, though
the outgrowth of the University Extension movement,
is designed to supply the need so widely felt of author-
ized books for study and reference both by students
and by the general public.

The aim of these Manuals is to educate rather
than to inform. In their preparation, details will be
avoided except when they illustrate the working of
general laws and the development of principles ; while
the historical evolution of both the literary and
scientific subjects, as well as their philosophical significance, will be kept in view.

The remarkable success which has attended University Extension in England has been largely due to
the union of scientific with popular treatment, and of
simplicity with thoroughness.

This movement, however, can only reach those
resident in the larger centres of population, while all
over the country there are thoughtful persons who

desire the same kind of teaching. It is for them also that this Series is designed. Its aim is to supply the general reader with the same kind of teaching as is given in lectures, and to reflect the spirit which has characterized the movement, viz., the combination of principles with facts and of methods with results.

The Manuals are also intended to be contributions to the literature of the subjects with which they respectively deal quite apart from University Extension; and some of them will be found to meet a general rather than a special want.

They will be issued simultaneously in England and America. Volumes dealing with separate sections of Literature, Science, Philosophy, History, and Art, have been assigned to representative literary men, to University Professors, or to Extension Lecturers connected with Oxford, Cambridge, London, and the Universities of Scotland and Ireland.

NOW READY

THE USE AND ABUSE OF MONEY

By Dr. W. CUNNINGHAM, Trinity College, Cambridge. 12mo, $1.00, *net.*

CONTENTS—POLITICAL ECONOMY WITH ASSUMPTIONS AND WITHOUT—INDUSTRY WITHOUT CAPITAL.— CAPITALIST ERA — MATERIAL PROGRESS AND MORAL INDIFFERENCE—THE CONTROL OF CAPITAL—THE FORMATION OF CAPITAL—THE INVESTMENT OF CAPITAL— CAPITAL IN ACTION — THE REPLACEMENT OF CAPITAL—THE DIRECTION OF CAPITAL—PERSONAL RESPONSI-BILITY—DUTY IN REGARD TO EMPLOYING CAPITAL—DUTY IN REGARD TO THE RETURNS ON CAPITAL—THE ENJOYMENT OF WEALTH.

Dr. Cunningham's book is intended for those who are already familiar with the outlines of the subject, and is meant to help them to think on topics about which everybody talks. It is essentially a popular treatise, and the headings of the three parts, Social Problems, Practical Questions, and Personal Duty, give a broad view of the large scope of the book. The subject is Capital in its relation to Social Progress, and the title emphasizes the element of personal responsibility that enters into the questions raised. The discussion is as thorough as it is practical, the author's main purpose being to enlighten the lay reader. The novelty of his point of view and the clearness of his style unite to make the book both interesting and valuable. The volume contains a syllabus of subjects and a list of books for reference for the use of those who may wish to pursue the study further.

THE FINE ARTS

By G. BALDWIN BROWN, Professor of Fine Arts in the University of Edinburgh. 12mo, with Illustrations, $1.00, *net*.

CONTENTS—Part I.—ART AS THE EXPRESSION OF POPULAR FEELINGS AND IDEALS:—THE BEGINNINGS OF ART—THE FESTIVAL IN ITS RELATION TO THE FORM AND SPIRIT OF CLASSICAL ART—MEDIÆVAL FLORENCE AND HER PAINTERS. Part II.—THE FORMAL CONDITIONS OF ARTISTIC EXPRESSION: — SOME ELEMENTS OF EFFECT IN THE ARTS OF FORM—THE WORK OF ART AS SIGNIFICANT — THE WORK OF ART AS BEAUTIFUL. Part III.—THE ARTS OF FORM :—ARCHITECTURAL BEAUTY IN RELATION TO CONSTRUCTION—THE CONVENTIONS OF SCULPTURE —PAINTING OLD AND NEW.

The whole field of the fine-arts of painting, sculpture and architecture, their philosophy, function and historic accomplishment, is covered in Professor Baldwin Brown's compact but exhaustive manual. The work is divided into three parts, the first considering art as the expression of popular feelings and ideas— a most original investigation of the origin and development of the aesthetic impulse ; the second discussing the formal conditions of artistic expression ; and the third treating the " arts of form " in their theory and practice and giving a luminous exposition of the significance of the great historic movements in architecture, sculpture and painting from the earliest times to the present.

THE PHILOSOPHY OF THE BEAUTIFUL

Being the Outlines of the History of Aesthetics. By WILLIAM KNIGHT, Professor of Philosophy in the University of St. Andrews. 12mo, $1.00, *net*.

CONTENTS — INTRODUCTORY — PREHISTORIC ORIGINS — ORIENTAL ART AND SPECULATION—THE PHILOSOPHY OF GREECE

—THE NEOPLATONISTS—THE GRAECO-ROMAN PERIOD—MEDIAE-
VALISM — THE PHILOSOPHY OF GERMANY — OF FRANCE — OF
ITALY—OF HOLLAND—OF BRITAIN—OF AMERICA.

Not content with presenting an historical sketch of past opinion and tendency on the subject of the Beautiful, Prof. Knight
shows how these philosophical theories have been evolved, how
they have been the outcome of social as well as of intellectual
causes, and have often been the product of obscure phenomena
in the life of a nation. Thus a deep human interest is given to
his synopsis of speculative thought on the subject of Beauty and
to his analysis of the art school corresponding to each period
from the time of the Egyptians down to the present day. He
traces the sequence of opinion in each country as expressed in its
literature and its art works, and shows how doctrines of art are
based upon theories of Beauty, and how these theories often have
their roots in the customs of society itself.

ENGLISH COLONIZATION AND EMPIRE

By ALFRED CALDECOTT, St. John's College, Cambridge. 12mo, with Maps and Diagrams, $1.00,
net.

CONTENTS—PIONEER PERIOD—INTERNATIONAL STRUGGLE
—DEVELOPMENT AND SEPARATION OF AMERICA—THE ENGLISH
IN INDIA—RECONSTRUCTION AND FRESH DEVELOPMENT—GOV-
ERNMENT OF THE EMPIRE—TRADE AND TRADE POLICY—SUPPLY
OF LABOR — NATIVE RACES—EDUCATION AND RELIGION—GEN-
ERAL REFLECTIONS—BOOKS OF REFERENCE.

The diffusion of European, and, more particularly, of English,
civilization over the face of the inhabited and habitable world is
the subject of this book. The treatment of this great theme covers
the origin and the historical, political, economical and ethnological
development of the English colonies, the moral, intellectual, industrial and social aspects of the question being also considered.
There is thus spread before the reader a bird's-eye view of the
British colonies, great and small, from their origin until the present
time, with a summary of the wars and other great events which
have occurred in the progress of this colonizing work, and with
a careful examination of some of the most important questions,
economical, commercial and political, which now affect the relation of the colonies and the parent nation The maps and diagrams are an instructive and valuable addition to the book.

THE LITERATURE OF FRANCE

By H. G. KEENE, Hon. M.A. Oxon. 12mo, $1.00, *net*.

CONTENTS—Introduction.—THE AGE OF INFANCY (*a*. Birth)—THE AGE OF INFANCY (*b*. Growth)—THE AGE OF ADOLESCENCE (Sixteenth Century)—THE AGE OF GLORY, Part I. POETRY, ETC.—THE AGE OF GLORY, Part II. PROSE—THE AGE OF REASON, Part I.—THE AGE OF REASON, Part II.— THE AGE OF 'NATURE'—SOURCES OF MODERN FRENCH LITERARY ART : POETRY—SOURCES OF PROSE FICTION—APPENDIX— INDEX.

"My first impressions are fully confirmed. The book is interesting and able. It would be difficult to compress into equal compass a more satisfactory or suggestive view of so great a subject. As an introductory text for schools and colleges or private readers I have seen nothing so good. The book deserves, and I hope will receive, a wide welcome."—EDWARD S. JOYNES, *Professor of Modern Languages, South Carolina College.*

THE REALM OF NATURE

An Outline of Physiography. By HUGH ROBERT MILL, D.Sc. Edin.; Fellow of the Royal Society of Edinburgh ; Oxford Lecturer. Maps and 68 Illustrations. 12mo, $1.50, *net*.

CONTENTS—STORY OF NATURE—SUBSTANCE OF NATURE —POWER OF NATURE—THE EARTH A SPINNING BALL—THE EARTH A PLANET—THE SOLAR SYSTEM AND UNIVERSE—THE ATMOSPHERE — ATMOSPHERIC PHENOMENA — CLIMATES — THE HYDROSPHERE—BED OF THE OCEANS—CRUST OF THE EARTH— ACTION OF WATER ON LAND—RECORD OF THE ROCKS— CONTINENTAL AREA—LIFE AND LIVING CREATURES—MAN IN NATURE—APPENDICES—INDEX.

"An excellent book, clear, comprehensive, and remarkably accurate. The standard errors that one has come to expect in one text-book after another are successfully avoided, and this indicates high and scholarly attainments on the part of the author, and a broad acquaintance with modern sources of scientific statements. . . . One who reaches a good understanding of the book may regard himself as having made a real advance in his education towards an appreciation of nature."—Professor W. M. DAVIS, *of Harvard.*

"Evidently prepared by one who understood his subject."—Professor JAMES D. DANA, *Yale.*

"Admirably adapted for High Schools, as also a reference book for teachers. I can commend it with pleasure." Professor S. W. WILLISTON.

THE STUDY OF ANIMAL LIFE

By J. Arthur Thomson, M.A., F.R.S.E., University of Edinburgh. 12mo, Illustrated, $1.50 *net*.

An original and comprehensive account of all animal life, save man. Such topics as the wealth of life on the earth, its distribution, the struggle for existence, the social and domestic life of animals, instinct, structure, heredity, influence of habit and surroundings, etc., are thoroughly discussed, though in a bright and interesting way, and with the fact constantly in mind that the book is a manual and not a cyclopædia or a special treatise.

"I have read it with great delight. It is an admirable work, giving a true view of the existing state and tendencies of zoology; and it possesses the rare merit of being an elementary work, written from the standpoint of the most advanced thought, and in a manner to be understood by the beginning student."—J. H. Comstock, *Professor of Entomology in Cornhill University, and in Leland Stanford Junior University.*

"An interesting and stimulating book, especially so for teachers. The style is clear and attractive, and the illustrations excellent. The views taken as to evolution and heredity are sound and broad."—A. S. Packard, *Professor of Zoology, Brown University.*

THE ELEMENTS OF ETHICS

An Introduction to Moral Philosophy. By J. H. Muirhead, M.A., Royal Holloway College, England. 12mo, $1.00 *net*; introduction price, 80 cents *net*.

Contents: Book I. The Science of Ethics: Problem of, Can there be a Science of, Scope of the Science—Book II. Moral Judgment: Object of, Standard of, Moral Law—Book III. Theories of the End: As Pleasure, As Self-sacrifice, Evolutionary Hedonism—Book IV. The End as Good: As Common Good, Forms of the Good—Book V. Moral Progress: Standard As Relative, As Progressive, As Ideal—Bibliography.

"With admirable clearness defines the fields, analyzes ethical phenomena, subjects theories of various schools to searching criticism, and builds up in logical fashion his own system. An idealist, . . . can render good reasons for the faith that is in him. Spirit tolerant, method scientific, style easy and graceful."—*Public Opinion.*

"The is no other introduction which can be recommended."
—*The Academy*, London.

Returnable examination copy to Instructors, with view to class use, at Introduction price.

THE EARTH'S HISTORY

An Introduction to Modern Geology. By R. D. ROBERTS,
M.A., Camb., D.Sc., Lond. With colored Maps and Illustrations. 12mo, $1.50 *net*.

The purpose of this volume is to furnish a sketch of the methods and
chief results of geological inquiry, such as a student, or a reader interested
in the subject for its own sake, would desire to obtain. It is shown that
Geology is not a mere description of rocks and fossils, but a history, and
the purpose of the geologist is to reconstruct from ancient fragmentary
remains the old conditions that characterized successive stages of development—in a word, to make out the life history of the earth. Some of the
problems are: the nature of the crust movements to which land-areas and
mountain ranges are due; what was the distribution of land and water when
each group of rocks was formed; what the extent and contour of the land
were, the condition of its surface and the forms of life; what the oceanic
conditions, depths, life inhabiting the water, nature and extent of the
materials brought down by rivers.

The records of this series of events are to be found in the successive
groups of rocks, and the chief object of this volume is to present in broad
outline results of geological research which throw light upon the structural
history of the earth, and the method by which that history is worked
out.

THE FRENCH REVOLUTION

By CHARLES E. MALLET, Balliol College, Oxford. 12mo,
$1.00 *net*.

CONTENTS: Introductory—I. Condition of France in the Eighteenth Cen-
tury—II. Last Years of the Ancient Regime—III. The Early Days of the
Revolution—IV. Labours of the Constituent Assembly—V. Parties and Poli-
ticians under the Constituent Assembly—VI The Rise of the Jacobin
Party—VII. Influence of the War upon the Revolution—VIII. Fall of the
Gironde—IX. The Jacobins in Power—X. The Struggle of Parties and
the Ascendency of Robespierre—XI. The Reaction—Tables of Dates—
Appendix of Books—Index.

This book has a special value to students and readers who do not own the
great works of such writers as De Tocqueville, Taine, Michelet, and Von Sybel;
for it summarizes what t .ese and other writers tell us. Mr. Mallet presents
economic and political aspects of society before the Revolution; attempts to
explain why the Revolution came; why the men who made it failed to attain
the liberty they so ardently desired, or to found the new order which they hoped
to see in France; by what arts and accidents, owing to what deeper causes, an
inconspicuous minority gradually grew into a victorious party; how external
circumstances kept the revolutionary fever up, and forced the Revolution forward. He undertakes to make clear the mystery of the time, the real character
and aims of the men who grasped the supreme power in 1793-4, who held it
with such a combination of energy and folly, of heroism and crime, and who
proceeded, through anarchy and terror, to experiment how social misery could
be extinguished and universal felicity attained, by drastic philosophic remedies,
applied by despots, and enforced by death. History offers no problem of more
surpassing interest, and none more perplexing or obscure.

THE PHYSIOLOGY OF THE SENSES

By John McKendrick, Professor of Physiology in the University of Glasgow, and Dr. Snodgrass, Physiological Laboratory, Glasgow. Many Illustrations. 12mo, $1.00 *net.*

1. Touch, Taste, and Smell.   2. The Sense of Sight.   3. Sound and Hearing.

CHAPTERS IN MODERN BOTANY

By Patrick Geddes, Professor of Botany, University College, Dundee. Illustrations. 12mo, $ *net.*

Contents: I. and II. Pitcher Plants—III. Other Insectivorous Plants, Difficulties and Criticisms—IV. and V. Movement and Nervous Action in Plants—VI. The Web of Life—VII. Relations between Plants and Animals—VIII. Spring and its Studies ; Geographical Distribution and World Landscapes ; Seedling and Bud—IX. Leaves—X. Suggestions and Further Study.

OUTLINES OF ENGLISH LITERATURE. By William Renton, University of St. Andrews. 12mo, $1.00 *net. Ready.*

LOGIC, INDUCTIVE AND DEDUCTIVE. By William Minto, University of Aberdeen. *Ready.*

THE PHILOSOPHY OF THE BEAUTIFUL. By William Knight, Professor of Philosophy, University of St. Andrews. Part II. *Ready.*

COMPARATIVE RELIGION. By Prof. Menzies, University of St. Andrews. *In preparation.*

THE ENGLISH NOVEL FROM ITS ORIGIN TO SIR WALTER SCOTT. By Prof. Raleigh, University College, Liverpool.

PROBLEMS OF POLITICAL ECONOMY. By M. E. Sadler, Senior Student of Christ Church, Oxford.

PSYCHOLOGY: A HISTORICAL SKETCH. By Prof. Seth, University of St. Andrews.

ENERGY IN NATURE. An Introduction to Physical Science. By John Cox, Trinity College, Cambridge.

THE HISTORY OF ASTRONOMY. By Arthur Berry, King's College, Cambridge.

Privileges of Examination, Introductory Prices, Regular Rates to Instructors, to Libraries, and to the Trade furnished on application. Full Descriptive Catalogue of these and many other distinguished text-books in all departments of education, sent free. Also Miscellaneous Catalogue of American and Foreign Publications. All current books promptly supplied. Special facilities for procuring such as are rare or scarce.

CHARLES SCRIBNER'S SONS,

Publishers, Importers, and Booksellers,

743–745 Broadway,   ·   ·   ·   ·   ·   New York City.